PURPLE MAJESTY

THE BALTIMORE RAVENS' CHAMPIONSHIP SEASON

THE BALTIMORE SUN
LIGHT FOR ALL

The Baltimore Sun Company, LLC

Timothy E. Ryan, Publisher, President and Chief Executive Officer

Mary J. Corey, Director of Content and Senior Vice President
Triffon G. Alatzas, Head of Digital Media

Ron Fritz, Head of Sports
Andy Knobel, Deputy Sports Editor, Book Editor
Monique Jones, Ravens Editor

Jay Judge, Head of Visuals
Robert Hamilton, Director of Photography, Book Photo Editor

Steve Gould and Jonas Shaffer, Book Copy Editors

Gene Sweeney Jr., Cover Photo
Lloyd Fox, Back Cover Photo

Peter J. Clark, Publisher
Molly Voorheis, Managing Editor
Nicky Brillowski, Book and Cover Design
Sam Schmidt, Advertising

ISBN: 978-0-9885458-2-3 (PB)
ISBN: 978-0-9885458-3-0 (HC)

Printed in the United States of America
KCI Sports Publishing   3340 Whiting Avenue, Suite 5   Stevens Point, WI 54481
Phone: 1-800-697-3756   Fax: 715-344-2668
www.kcisports.com

CONTENTS

CHAMPIONS

WHAT A RIDE!

BY KEVIN COWHERD, THE BALTIMORE SUN

Twists, turns, highs, lows, a fourth–and–29 and a Flacco fling on the road to a Super Bowl title

It's the story of a proud football team that mirrors the city in which it plays, a hard-nosed, blue-collar bunch that overcame injury and adversity and went on a magical roll to reach the NFL's grandest stage.

It's a story weighted with dramatic subplots, too, from the death of a beloved owner to the "last ride" of perhaps the greatest defensive player the sport has ever seen to two brothers coaching against each other in the biggest game of their lives.

And when the final chapter was written, the Ravens stood on a podium in the Mercedes-Benz Superdome in New Orleans and hoisted the gleaming Vince Lombardi Trophy, 34-31 winners over the San Francisco 49ers in Super Bowl XLVII.

What a season it was. Twelve years after winning pro football's biggest prize, the Ravens did it again after a tough little running back named Ray Rice proclaimed it was their destiny. And who could argue with that after all the ups and downs this team went through?

The downs started as early as April. On the final day of the NFL draft, the Ravens learned that Terrell Suggs, their sublime pass rusher and reigning NFL Defensive Player of the Year, had torn

Owner Steve Bisciotti raises the Lombardi Trophy as coach John Harbaugh looks on after the Ravens' Super Bowl XLVII victory over the 49ers. The championship was the team's first since January 2001.
Gene Sweeney Jr. | Baltimore Sun Photo

Wide receiver Torrey Smith points skyward after his second-quarter touchdown reception against the Patriots on Sept. 23. Smith learned earlier in the day that his brother, Tevin, had died in a motorcycle accident.
Karl Merton Ferron | Baltimore Sun Photo

his right Achilles tendon.

Reports indicated that Suggs injured himself playing basketball back home in Arizona. But the voluble linebacker insisted that he'd hurt himself doing conditioning drills. Even with Suggs bragging that he'd return by October or November, a pall settled over Ravens Nation.

In training camp, a new storyline emerged: a gutty free-agent rookie named Justin Tucker was challenging veteran Billy Cundiff for the kicking job.

Ravens coach John Harbaugh had publicly backed Cundiff after he shanked a chip-shot field-goal attempt in the waning seconds of the Ravens' shocking loss to the New England Patriots in the AFC championship game a year earlier.

Nevertheless, Tucker was brought in to give Cundiff competition. Tucker's slight build and choir-boy features masked a powerful foot and the nerves of a cat burglar. In late August, Cundiff was cut and Tucker would go on to have a brilliant rookie season, connecting on 30 of 33 field-goal attempts — the second-best regular-season mark in Ravens history.

September was a month of loss for the Ravens — at least off the playing field.

Art Modell, who had brought the franchise to Baltimore from Cleveland amid much controversy and personal angst, died at age 87. Modell was a cheerful visionary who had helped negotiate the league's first collective bargaining agreement with the players. And he was the driving force in the first TV deals between the league and the networks that helped the NFL's popularity skyrocket.

To commemorate their cherished former owner, the Ravens wore a uniform patch that read simply "Art" for the rest of the season.

Two weeks later, on a Sunday morning, wide receiver Torrey Smith learned that his 19-year-old brother, Tevin, was dead in a motorcycle crash in Virginia.

Though wracked with grief, Smith decided to play that night against the New England Patriots at M&T Bank Stadium. And when he made the first of his two touchdown receptions — on a 25-yard lob from quarterback Joe Flacco in the left corner of the end zone — the stadium exploded with noise as Smith went to one knee and pointed to the heavens.

By the time he reached the sideline and slumped on the bench, he was in tears. And when the game was over, one by one, his teammates embraced him and reminded him his Ravens family was there for him, too.

October was a month of more emotional swings for the Ravens. In a 31-29 win over the Dallas Cowboys at the Bank, linebacker Ray Lewis, their undisputed leader for 17 years, tore his right triceps. The all-but-certain Hall of Famer was thought to be out for the season.

But Terrell Suggs shocked Ravens Nation — and the rest of the NFL — by making good on his promise and returning for the road game against the Houston Texans late in the month. It was a deflating 43-13 loss. But Suggs, despite showing rust and 10 extra pounds, played effec-

Nose tackle Terrence Cody looks on as linebacker Terrell Suggs (55) celebrates a sack of the Texans' Matt Schaub on Oct. 21. It was Suggs' first game since suffering a torn Achilles tendon in April. *Karl Merton Ferron | Baltimore Sun Photo*

Running back Ray Rice lunges for a first down as Chargers cornerbacks Quentin Jammer (23) and Antoine Cason bring him down. Rice gained 29 yards on a fourth-and-29 check-down pass as the Ravens won in overtime on Nov. 25.
Karl Merton Ferron | Baltimore Sun Photo

tively and with unbridled joy, giving the team a lift it sorely needed.

With the redoubtable Suggs back in the lineup, the Ravens rattled off four more wins for a 9-2 start. The final game of that stretch was a heart-stopper. On the Sunday after Thanksgiving, trailing the San Diego Chargers in the fourth quarter at Qualcomm Stadium, Ray Rice set off on an electrifying 29-yard catch-and-run on fourth-and-29 to keep the Ravens' hopes alive en route to a 16-13 overtime win.

It was their last bit of good fortune for a while.

Three straight dispiriting losses ensued — to the archrival Pittsburgh Steelers, Washington Redskins and Denver Broncos. Concerned about their lethargic running and passing attacks, the Ravens fired offensive coordinator Cam Cameron in a surprise move after the Redskins game and replaced him with quarterbacks coach Jim Caldwell.

Finishing the regular season with a 10-6 mark, the AFC North title and a playoff berth for the fifth straight year, the Ravens were buoyed by the return of Lewis for their wild-card game against the Indianapolis Colts. In a bombshell announcement four days earlier, No. 52 had said he was retiring at the end of the season, calling it his "last ride."

But after emerging from the tunnel and doing his signature "Squirrel" pregame dance for the last time in front of a roaring crowd at the Bank, Lewis recorded a game-high 13 tackles and helped lead the Ravens to a 24-9 win.

Now it was on to Denver and a divisional-round game against the masterful Peyton Manning and the Broncos. At frozen Sports Authority Field, the teams hooked up in a game for the ages. In a wild play near the end of regulation, Joe Flacco launched a Hail Mary down the right sideline and connected with Jacoby

Above: Jim Caldwell takes the field with quarterback Joe Flacco before facing the Broncos on Dec. 16. Caldwell was promoted to replace fired offensive coordinator Cam Cameron six days earlier. *Gene Sweeney Jr. | Baltimore Sun Photo*

Left: Flacco celebrates his desperation 70-yard pass to Jacoby Jones that sent the divisional game against the Broncos into overtime Jan. 12. *Gene Sweeney Jr. | Baltimore Sun Photo*

Jones for a 70-yard touchdown over a stumbling Denver safety. And in the second quarter of overtime, Tucker drilled a 47-yard field for a frenetic 38-35 Ravens win.

Now the Ravens were right where they wanted to be, with a rematch against the Patriots in Foxborough, Mass., for the AFC championship. Revenge was sweet. The Ravens defense stared down New England quarterback Tom Brady in the second half, and Flacco was masterful for the third straight game, completing 21 of 36 passes for 240 yards and three touchdowns in the Ravens' 28-13 victory.

From there it was on to New Orleans and the much-hyped HarBowl, with John Harbaugh and his brother, Jim, the 49ers coach, matching wits from opposite sidelines to make NFL history.

What a "last ride" it was for Lewis, too, who insisted all along he had his sights set on only one goal throughout this wonderful season.

"The real prize," No. 52 said over and over, "is actually going and winning the Super Bowl."

And now, with the Lombardi Trophy back in Baltimore, the Ravens have done just that.■

Players watch retiring linebacker Ray Lewis perform his pregame dance before his last home game, the wildcard victory over the Colts on Jan. 6. *Gene Sweeney Jr. | Baltimore Sun Photo*

ART MODELL

BY MIKE PRESTON, THE BALTIMORE SUN

Beloved owner lived for 3 passions: his family, the NFL, his team

The new Ravens owner was sitting on stage at the Inner Harbor and looking quite uncomfortable. On Nov. 6, 1995, Art Modell announced that he was moving the Browns from Cleveland to Baltimore, and while local politicians couldn't hide their enthusiasm, Modell appeared embarrassed.

Seconds after the news conference ended, Modell was ushered off the stage like the president of the United States, completely surrounded by security. But he left his limousine window open for a few seconds, so I approached to introduce myself, only to have him roll the window up in my face.

There couldn't have been a more inauspicious start. Little did I realize then that this was the beginning of a long relationship with a man who embodied the NFL and had two other great passions — his family and his team.

Art Modell and I weren't great friends. We never went out to dinner, and our families didn't share time together. We were just two people who shared a deep, mutual respect. We stayed in contact up until his death Sept. 6, long after Steve Bisciotti became the majority owner of the Ravens in April 2004.

The NFL has lost one of its greatest statesmen.

It's impossible to talk about the history of the league without mentioning the contributions of Modell. His legacy is as great as those of some of the other NFL's storied men, such as Wellington Mara and George Halas. Modell embodied the game from the days of Blanton Collier and Jim Brown to the times of Ray Lewis and Jonathan Ogden.

He won NFL championships in 1964 and 2000, but Modell loved his family more than football. He adored his wife, Pat. He might have been the owner, but we all knew who the boss was. He spent countless hours talking about his grandchildren and actually con-

Above is a patch the Ravens wore this season in Art Modell's memory.
Gene Sweeney Jr. | Baltimore Sun Photo

fessed to me once how miserable his life had become when one of his sons got divorced years ago. Modell was criticized for being greedy when he moved the Browns from Cleveland to Baltimore, but he knew that was the only way he could set up his family financially before he died.

Family and football, though, often went hand in hand. Modell took losses personally.

"This is an embarrassment to myself, Pat, and the entire Modell family," Modell would say after lopsided losses. At first, we used to joke about the statement only to learn later he was serious.

Modell's teams were an extension of his family. He had affection for former Ravens coach Ted Marchibroda and cried when he fired him. I'll never forget how Modell broke down when I told him that middle linebacker Ray Lewis had been arrested at an Atlanta airport because of an alleged involvement in a double murder. Critics said Modell fought for Lewis only because he was the team's star player, but they were so very wrong.

Modell always gave his players a second chance. Ask Ravens executive vice president/general manager Ozzie Newsome or Hall of Fame running back Jim Brown. When players asked him for personal favors, he delivered. When a member of Michael McCrary's family needed medical attention, Modell sent out a chartered jet and made sure that person was seen by some of the nation's top doctors.

His Inner Circle program, developed in Cleveland, was an in-house organization that helped his players overcome financial problems as well as alcohol and drug addictions. Modell liked being tight with the players.

That was his strength, but also his weakness. He often bailed players out of trouble or lent them money, and that cost him millions of dollars. Once I got into a major fight with Modell because I wrote a column criticizing him for letting defensive tackle

Former Ravens majority owner Art Modell moved the franchise to Baltimore for the 1996 season. He died Sept. 6. *Gene Sweeney Jr. | Baltimore Sun Photo 2011*

Larry Webster back on the team after he violated the league's substance-and-alcohol-abuse policy for the fourth time.

When Modell pointed his finger at you and called you "young man," it was no longer an argument, but a monologue.

"Listen here, young man," he said. "I never give up on my players, and I'll never give up on people. That's the way I have always been and I will remain that way. Do you understand me, young man?" he asked as he hung up the phone.

Former Cleveland coach Bill Belichick, now with the New England Patriots, once told me that you could harshly criticize Modell one day, and the next day he would be your best friend.

He was right. The next morning, Modell walked into the media room, shook my hand and kissed me on the cheek. He was happy, just as long as he was in the world of pro football. He was a throwback owner who had no other businesses. He frequently attended practices despite the bitter cold or sizzling heat. When he became too old to walk, he was driven around in a golf cart.

The players liked seeing Modell on the sideline. The Ravens wanted to win the Super Bowl in the 2000 season just as much for the "old man" as they did for themselves. They loved Modell because they knew he had a big heart, and in it there was a special place for them and the league. As the ultimate league guy, he never publicly complained about not getting into the Pro Football Hall of Fame even though he belonged there.

His record is impeccable. He helped launch "Monday Night Football." Along with late league commissioner Pete Rozelle, they worked closely together in establishing NFL Films. Modell was chairman of the Owners Labor Committee in 1968, when it negotiated the NFL's first collective bargaining agreement.

Modell's record is unmatched when it came to hiring minorities in the front office, and the NFL certainly wouldn't be the No. 1 sports league in the world today if it weren't for Modell negotiating TV contracts from 1962 through 1993.

He'll get into the Hall of Fame, but it's a shame that it will be posthumously. For people like myself, a more fitting tribute is the huge portrait of Modell at the entrance to the Ravens' training facility in Owings Mills. Modell is dressed in a charcoal-colored, doubled-breasted suit, and both his hands are in his famous camel overcoat. Modell looks distinguished and honorable, and seems to welcome any football fan to his world, one that consisted of three passions: his family, the NFL and his team.■

SEPTEMBER 10, 2012	1	2	3	4	F
BENGALS	0	10	3	0	13
RAVENS	10	7	17	10	44

OFF TO A FLYING START

BY JEFF ZREBIEC, THE BALTIMORE SUN

From the very first play from scrimmage, no-huddle offense delivers in an opening-game rout

For the past six weeks, the Ravens had seen this from Joe Flacco on a daily basis.

They watched him fit throws into the tightest of spaces and hit receivers in stride 50 yards downfield. They marveled at his calmness and command of the huddle.

So while a "Monday Night Football" national television audience was introduced to a new-look offense and a confident quarterback at the top of his game, the Ravens simply got confirmation of something they had been witnessing for weeks.

From his first pass, a 52-yard bomb to Torrey Smith (Maryland) on the game's first play from scrimmage, until he gave way to backup quarterback Tyrod Taylor midway through the fourth quarter of a 44-13 rout of the Cincinnati Bengals, Flacco was in complete command.

Flacco completed 21 of 29 passes for 299 yards, two touchdowns and no interceptions Monday, and the Ravens scored the game's final 27 points to begin the season 1-0 for the fifth time under coach John Harbaugh. The 44 points tied for the third-most

Ravens linebacker Ray Lewis and Olympic gold-medal swimmer Michael Phelps of Baltimore share their thoughts before the regular-season opener.
Lloyd Fox | Baltimore Sun Photo

that the Ravens have ever scored in the regular season.

"It was a lot of fun — you can't lie about that," Flacco said. "We didn't get that many drives, really, but we were efficient enough that we put points on the board, and sometimes that's what you need to do."

In blowing out the Bengals in front of an announced 71,064 at

M&T Bank Stadium, the Ravens won their 12th straight home game. The Ravens, who swept the division en route to the AFC North title last season, have won nine straight games against divisional foes, an NFL high.

For a little while, the streak looked to be in jeopardy. The Ravens' lead was down from 14

Wide receiver Torrey Smith catches a first-quarter pass from Joe Flacco as Bengals cornerback Leon Hall flies in to defend. *Lloyd Fox | Baltimore Sun Photo*

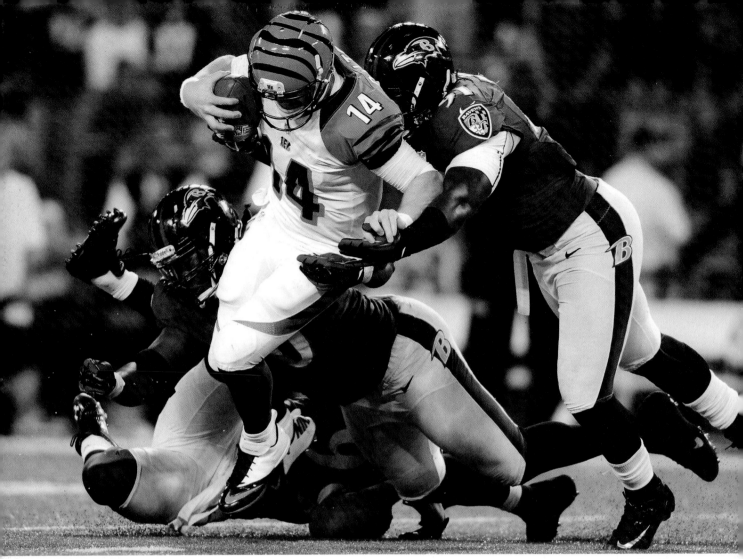

Bengals quarterback Andy Dalton is sacked by a host of Ravens during the fourth quarter. Dalton was sacked four times, three of them in the fourth quarter. *Christopher T. Assaf | Baltimore Sun Photo*

points to four in the third quarter, and the defense was struggling to contain quarterback Andy Dalton and running back BenJarvus Green-Ellis.

That's when Flacco got his hands back on the ball and put the Bengals away. Thriving in the no-huddle offense, Flacco hit tight end Dennis Pitta for a 10-yard touchdown pass that made it an 11-point game.

The next drive ended with a 40-yard field goal from rookie Justin Tucker, who converted all three of his field-goal attempts and all five of his extra points.

Safety Ed Reed intercepted an errant pass by Dalton on the Bengals' next possession and returned it 34 yards for a touchdown. If Reed's score didn't officially put the Bengals away,

then Ray Rice's second touchdown, this one from 1 yard after Ray Lewis caused Dalton to fumble, most certainly did.

"You always want to come out fast in the first one," said Rice, who rushed for 68 yards and the two touchdowns on 10 carries and caught three passes for 25 yards. "Our offense is real explosive. I think this is the fastest group we've had since I've been here."

The Ravens accumulated 430 total yards of offense as Flacco worked in a little of everything. Eight players caught passes, and seven carried the ball. Flacco orchestrated it all, showing great arm strength on deep passes to Smith to start the game and to Anquan Boldin on a 34-yard touchdown strike between two defenders early in the second

quarter.

Then he exhibited great touch and poise, holding his ground in the face of a blitz and throwing a jump ball to Pitta, who soared over Leon Hall for the touchdown that made it a 24-13 game at the 5:18 mark of the third quarter.

"We've always stood up here, and we've always, all our coaches, the organization, we know what we've got in this guy," said Harbaugh, who agreed with a reporter's assessment that his quarterback could be "scary good" this season.

"Of course he is [elite]. He is a winner. He is one of the toughest quarterbacks I have ever been around. He's the best quarterback I've ever been around."

Harbaugh then took it a step

Fans behind the end zone at M&T Bank Stadium yell at the Bengals offense as it nears the goal line in the third quarter. The Ravens held Cincinnati to a field goal on the drive. *Christopher T. Assaf | Baltimore Sun Photo*

further when asked whether Flacco, who is in the final season of his contract and whose agent has been negotiating a contract extension with the Ravens since February, just raised his price tag.

"Pay him whatever he wants," Harbaugh said as he broke out into laughter. "Pay the man."

Flacco, who was standing about 5 yards away from the podium, added: "Hey, you all heard that. ... I don't concern myself with that stuff. I feel like I always go out there, and we go out on the field, and we play pretty [darn] good every week. The stats might not always say 299 yards or 300 yards or 450 yards. But the bottom line is I go out there, and I play hard, I play tough and we win a lot of football games around here."

It was that kind of night for the Ravens, who appeared to be in control of the game after Boldin's touchdown gave them a 17-3 lead.

However, relying on quick strikes from Dalton to A.J. Green and Andrew Hawkins and the hard running of Green-Ellis, Cincinnati marched 81 yards on 18 plays just before halftime, converting twice on fourth down. On fourth-and-1 from the 6-yard line, Green-Ellis powered his way in for the score to cut

the Ravens' lead to 17-10.

Cincinnati got the ball back to start the second half and again marched right down the field to first-and-goal.

However, Green-Ellis was stopped for 1 yard on first down, Dalton threw incomplete on second down and then tried to run it in on third down, but he was stopped on the 1-yard line by a combination of Lewis, Reed and Albert McClellan.

Cincinnati was forced to settle for Mike Nugent's 19-yard field goal that cut the Ravens' advantage to 17-13. That was about the last time the Bengals offense even threatened.

Dalton was sacked four times, two by defensive tackle Haloti Ngata. Lewis had 14 tackles and a forced fumble, and cornerback Lardarius Webb had seven tackles and a fumble recovery. But on this night, they were plenty content to play a supporting role to Flacco.

"Joe has gotten better every year," Reed said. "This is what we've seen all camp with Joe, just throwing the ball to those guys, putting it right in their chest, putting it right on their hands. You see that. Those guys trust him and want to make plays for him." ∎

SEPTEMBER 16, 2012	1	2	3	4	F
RAVENS	7	10	0	6	23
EAGLES	7	0	10	7	24

LETTING VICTORY PASS BY

BY JEFF ZREBIEC, THE BALTIMORE SUN

With Ravens up 10 points at half, the running game disap–pears — and so do chances for a win

PHILADELPHIA — When his final pass sailed over Ray Rice's head and hit the turf at Lincoln Financial Field, Ravens quarterback Joe Flacco threw his hands up, seemingly in desperation and disbelief.

The gesture was symbolic in a 24-23 loss Sunday to the Philadelphia Eagles in front of an announced 69,144, a defeat that revived long-standing second-guessing about the offensive play-calling and left several prominent Ravens blasting the replacement officials.

Eagles quarterback Michael Vick plunged in from the 1-yard line for the go-ahead score with 1:55 left in the fourth quarter and the Ravens' final drive stalled at their 46 when they chose to throw the ball on back-to-back plays when all they needed was a yard for a first down.

Under duress throughout the day, Flacco sailed both throws over the heads of his intended receivers. A week after a near-flaw-less performance in a beat-down of the Cincinnati Bengals, Flacco finished 22-for-42 for 232 yards, one touchdown and one intercep-

Ravens fan Eric Hall watches, not happily, as the Eagles go up 7-0 on LeSean McCoy's first-quarter run. *Gene Sweeney Jr.* | *Baltimore Sun Photo*

tion. He was just 8-for-25 in the second half, when the Ravens saw leads of 17-7 and 23-17 disappear in their first loss of the season.

"I wish I would have just scrambled around a little bit," Flacco said of his final ill-fated throw. "I threw my arms up, yeah. Maybe there was a little contact when the ball was in the air. I was just trying to get something crazy to happen. ... I was just hoping."

That's all the Ravens could do

after a game they lost despite forcing four turnovers and getting 152 total yards of offense from Ray Rice and three clutch field goals from Justin Tucker, who tied Wade Richey's team record by converting a 56-yard field goal just before halftime.

Tucker broke a 17-all tie with a 51-yard field goal at the 11:28 mark of the fourth quarter. A little over six minutes later, the undrafted rookie free agent out

of Texas converted from 48 yards, increasing the lead to 23-17 with 4:43 to play.

However, Vick, who overcame two interceptions and two Eagles fumbles deep in Ravens territory, used 10 plays to drive his team 80 yards for the go-ahead score. He hit wide receiver DeSean Jackson for 13 yards, tight end Brent Celek on passes of 24 yards and 13 yards, and tight end Clay Harbor for 19 yards. He then finished the drive by taking it himself from a yard out.

Finding holes in a defense that lost safety Bernard Pollard to a rib injury late in the first quarter, Vick completed 23 of 32 passes for 371 yards with one touchdown, and he ran for 34 yards and a touchdown.

"He can beat us in many ways, but we made the plays we were supposed to make," Ravens inside linebacker Ray Lewis said of Vick. "For us to come in and get four turnovers, when you got somebody down, put them away. Don't leave a team [hanging] around."

Lewis then expressed his displeasure with the replacement referees and called for the NFL to settle the dispute with the regular officials.

"It's nothing about them, per se. We're not directly attacking them. But we are saying we need the guys that do their regular jobs," Lewis said. "The time is now. How much longer are we going to keep going through this process? I just know across the league, teams are being affected by that. If they want the league to have the same reputation it always had, then address the problem. Get the regular referees in

Quarterback Joe Flacco walks off the field after the Ravens' 24-23 loss. Flacco was 22-for-42 for 232 yards with one touchdown pass and one interception. *Gene Sweeney Jr. | Baltimore Sun Photo*

here and let the games play themselves out. We should address it."

Lewis was miffed by the reversal of what was originally called a fumble by Vick on the play that preceded his decisive running touchdown. Haloti Ngata drilled the quarterback, who appeared to throw the ball away before hitting the ground. The officials initially ruled it was a fumble and rewarded the Ravens the ball. However, their call was overturned, which appeared to be the right decision.

That was one of many gripes for the Ravens. Coach John Harbaugh later described the game, which included multiple altercations and stoppages, as "chaotic."

"The challenge for us right now is what constitutes what," Harbaugh said. "What constitutes illegal contact, what constitutes pass interference, I'm not sure right now."

Harbaugh was referring in part to an offensive pass interference call on wide receiver Jacoby Jones that took away what would have been a 25-yard touchdown. The play, in which Jones outmaneuvered Nnamdi Asomugha in the end zone for the second time, would have given the Ravens a 27-17 lead with just over five minutes to play. Instead, they settled for Tucker's 48-yard field goal.

"He didn't even throw a flag," Flacco said. "He threw a blue beanie and then put his hands in the air like offensive pass interference. Come on."

Still, it never should have gotten to the point where calls were perceived as a potential difference in the game. The Ravens had control of the game with a 10-point lead and the ball early in the third quarter. However, Flacco threw an interception on the first possession of the second half, and Vick turned it into a 23-yard touchdown pass to Jeremy Maclin.

Wide receiver Jacoby Jones catches a 21-yard touchdown pass from Joe Flacco to put the Ravens up 14-7 in the second quarter.
Kenneth K. Lam | Baltimore Sun Photo

The Ravens then went three-and-out on their next three drives as Rice, who rushed seven times for 78 yards in the first half, curiously turned into a decoy. After his 16-yard run at the 2:11 mark of the second quarter, Rice didn't take another handoff from Flacco until the 5:30 mark of the third quarter. The Ravens ran 12 offensive plays between the carries and gained 29 total yards, with Flacco throwing his interception.

"We ran the plays that were called. I think we left a lot of plays on the field. They made more plays when they had to, and we didn't," said Rice, who finished with 16 carries for 99 yards and six catches for 53 yards. "I don't feel like [the running game] was abandoned. I feel

Linebackers Albert McClellan (50) and Ray Lewis walk back to the sideline as Eagles quarterback Michael Vick, top, celebrates his go-ahead 1-yard touchdown plunge with 1:55 left. *Gene Sweeney Jr. | Baltimore Sun Photo*

like we had to do what we had to do. This new tempo offense, I'm never going to be the guy. My thing is always touches. As long as they find ways to get me the ball, that would be great. We were running the ball really well today."

The Ravens rushed for 111 total yards and averaged 5.3 yards per carry. However, their undoing was going 4-for-14 on third down and 0-for-2 on fourth down.

"We just have to find a way to stay on the field on third down," said fullback Vonta Leach, who had a 5-yard touchdown run in the first quarter, his first points as a Raven. "For whatever reason, we weren't good on third downs."

The Ravens had six opportunities of 2 yards or less on third or fourth down that could have prolonged drives. Each time, they passed and did not pick up the first down. That, more than anything else, might have been the difference in entering the AFC championship game rematch Sunday against the New England Patriots off a brutal loss rather than an uplifting win.

"We'll probably go back and look and see if there's some things we could have done there just because they were doing a good job in their coverage and things like that," Flacco said. "The bottom line is, we have to execute and we weren't able to."∎

SEPTEMBER 23, 2012	1	2	3	4	F
PATRIOTS	13	7	7	3	30
RAVENS	0	14	7	10	31

THE SHOE IS ON THE OTHER FOOT

BY JEFF ZREBIEC, THE BALTIMORE SUN

Rookie kicker Tucker avoids Cundiff's fate, barely making game–winning field goal

This time, the late-game heartbreak belonged to the New England Patriots as wide left turned into just right.

Rookie kicker Justin Tucker barely kept a 27-yard field goal inside the right upright as time expired to give the Ravens a frantic 31-30 comeback victory Sunday night in front of an announced 71,269 at M&T Bank Stadium.

"What would be a better story than the one you saw?" Ravens coach John Harbaugh asked.

Trailing by nine points with 7 minutes, 29 seconds to play, Joe Flacco led a drive that culminated with a 5-yard touchdown pass to Torrey Smith with 4:01 on the clock, and the Ravens' fifth-year quarterback then led another drive in the final two minutes to set up Tucker for the game-winner.

Just eight months after Billy Cundiff missed a 32-yard field-goal attempt at Gillette Stadium that would have likely sent the AFC championship game against the Patriots into overtime, Tucker converted, giving the Ravens the victory. Twice they erased double-digit deficits in the game.

The win left Smith, who learned earlier in the day that his younger brother, Tevin Jones, had died in a motorcycle crash, leaping up and down on the sideline and then clutching the

Wide receiver Torrey Smith, a Maryland alumnus whose brother Tevin died in a motorcycle crash a day earlier, wipes his eye after the national anthem. *Karl Merton Ferron | Baltimore Sun Photo*

game ball as he exited the field. Harbaugh, meanwhile, stood on the bench, exhorting the fans.

"Our team just fights. We just have a bunch of guys that will not quit," the coach said. "I couldn't be more proud of the football team."

Patriots coach Bill Belichick ran onto the field and tried to grab the arm of an official after the game, which featured several controversial calls and 218 total yards on 24 penalties, 10 of them called on New England. Several Patriots also protested that Tucker's field goal was called good, but the

Safety Ed Reed pushes Patriots wide receiver Deion Branch out of bounds after an 11-yard reception on the Patriots' scoring drive late in the second quarter. *Kenneth K. Lam | Baltimore Sun Photo*

play was not reviewed.

"I'm not going to comment on that," Belichick said when asked about the officiating. "You saw the game. What did we have, 30 penalties called in that game?"

All that mattered to the Ravens (2-1) was that they extended their NFL-best home winning streak to 11 games and that they beat the Patriots for the first time in a regular-season game in seven tries. They will play host to the Cleve-

land Browns on Thursday night.

"It just means we're 2-1 and not 1-2, and we can move on to Cleveland a little bit quicker than if it would have went the other way," Flacco said.

Flacco, who was on point for much of the night, got the ball back at his 20 with 1:55 left after a rare stop by the Ravens defense against Tom Brady's offense. A 24-yard pass to Jacoby Jones, a 17-yard completion to tight end

Dennis Pitta, and a pass-interference call against Devin McCourty on Jones got the ball to the Patriots 7. Flacco knelt and put the game on Tucker's foot with two seconds to go.

"It kind of goes back to something I've been saying, something I've been trying to stick to: I try to treat every kick the same way," said Tucker, who is 7-for-7 on field-goal attempts this season. "In that regard, I'm happy with the end result. It was good and the Ravens win, so just mission accomplished."

Flacco was 28-for-39 for 382 yards, three touchdowns and an interception in one of the finest performances of his career. He spread the ball around as five Ravens had three catches or more, but he had the most success throwing to Smith.

The second-year receiver caught six balls for 127 yards and two touchdowns, ending an emotional day for him and his family. Smith, who left the team early Sunday morning after learning of his brother's accident, didn't decide that he was going to play until a couple of hours before kickoff.

"Emotionally, I didn't know how I would hold up," said Smith, who celebrated his first touchdown, a 25-yard catch in the second quarter, by getting down on one knee and then pointing to the sky. "I was telling my teammates a minute ago that this was new territory for me personally. I never had to deal with a death in my family. Obviously, you play with a heavy heart and you want to play for that person."

Brady finished 28 of 41 for 335 yards, one touchdown and no interceptions, Wes Welker caught eight passes for 142 yards, and Brandon Lloyd had nine catches for 108 yards. Frequently picking on the Ravens pass defense and specifically targeting cornerback Cary Williams, Brady led three straight scoring drives. His 7-yard touchdown pass to Julian Edelman just seconds before halftime allowed the Patriots to head into intermission with a 20-14 lead.

He then answered a 7-yard touchdown run from Ray Rice, who finished with 101 rushing yards and five catches for 49 yards, with a 12-play, 80-yard drive that ended on Danny Woodhead's 3-yard touchdown run.

Tight end Dennis Pitta, left, and quarterback Joe Flacco celebrate Pitta's 20-yard touchdown reception in the second quarter.
Gene Sweeney Jr. | Baltimore Sun Photo

Quarterback Joe Flacco, who went 28-for-39 for 382 yards and three touchdowns, runs for a second-quarter first down. *Gene Sweeney Jr. | Baltimore Sun Photo*

A 20-yard field goal by Stephen Gostkowski on the Patriots' next possession extended the visitors' lead to 30-21. But the final two Patriots drives ended with punts, opening the door for the comeback, which started with Smith's touchdown catch at 4:08 of the fourth quarter. The drive covered 92 yards in eight plays and included two big penalties on the Patriots.

"There's not a better person on this team than Torrey Smith, and to come out tonight and play the way he did with all that adversity and turmoil in his life right now, the guy is unbelievable," Pitta said. "Enough can't be said about him."

After the first quarter, the Ravens had been outgained 143-21. They ran only nine plays to the Patriots' 24, and they had no first downs to New England's six. They were probably lucky they were down only 13-0. At that point, late in the first quarter, the Ravens still didn't have a first down.

They finally got one on their next drive, thanks to defensive pass interference. That spearheaded a long drive that included a clutch 14-yard pass from Flacco to veteran wide receiver Anquan Boldin on third-and-13. Rice then rattled off runs of 8 and 5 yards before Flacco hit Smith with a 25-yard touchdown pass in the left corner of the end zone.

Trailing 13-7, the Ravens got the ball back and Flacco led another extended drive. A 41-yard pass to Jones put the ball in New England territory. Two runs by Rice advanced it to the 20, where Flacco hit Pitta on the right side. The tight end broke an arm tackle by McCourty and hurdled a lunging Gregory to score from 20 yards out and give the Ravens a 14-13 lead.

However, it was short-lived. Brady got the ball back at his 19 and with 1:41 on the clock. He hit Rob Gronkowski for 12 yards and then found Deion Branch for 11 to get the ball in Ravens territory. A 28-yard completion to Welker got the ball to the 7. On second-and-7 from the 7 with seven seconds to play, Edelman found a space between linebacker Dannell Ellerbe and safety Bernard Pollard and caught a touchdown pass.

That allowed the Patriots to take a 20-14 lead into halftime.■

SCORING SUMMARY

1st Quarter
7:12	NE	FG	Gostkowski 37
7:51	NE	TD	Bolden 2 run (Gostkowski kick)
14:22	NE	FG	Gostkowski 49

2nd Quarter
5:15	Bal	TD	T. Smith 25 pass from Flacco (Tucker kick)
13:13	Bal	TD	Pitta 20 pass from Flacco (Tucker kick)
14:58	NE	TD	Edelman 7 pass from Brady (Gostkowski kick)

3rd Quarter
| 3:24 | Bal | TD | Rice 7 run (Tucker kick) |
| 8:12 | NE | TD | Woodhead 3 run (Gostkowski kick) |

4th Quarter
0:50	NE	FG	Gostkowski 20
10:59	Bal	TD	T. Smith 5 pass from Flacco (Tucker kick)
15:00	Bal	FG	Tucker 27

SEPTEMBER 27, 2012	1	2	3	4	F
BROWNS	0	7	3	6	16
RAVENS	0	9	14	0	23

KEY PICK BY PICKED-ON WILLIAMS

BY JEFF ZREBIEC, THE BALTIMORE SUN

63-yard interception return late in third quarter helps Ravens weather the storm

For much of the first three weeks, opposing quarterbacks had found Ravens cornerback Cary Williams. They watched where he lined up and often threw in that direction.

But with the Ravens holding a precarious six-point lead late in the third quarter Thursday night, Cleveland Browns rookie quarterback Brandon Weeden lost sight of Williams. The result was the game's decisive play. Williams stepped in front of wide receiver Travis Benjamin in the flat and took the ball back 63 yards for a touchdown, his first career interception helping the Ravens turn aside the pesky Browns, 23-16, before an announced 70,944 at M&T Bank Stadium in a game played in a steady rainstorm.

"It's a once-in-a-lifetime opportunity. I was glad I was able to recognize the route and the formation, and I was glad to make the play," Williams said.

The interception gave the Ravens a 23-10 lead, which was ultimately whittled to seven on two 50-plus-yard field goals by veteran Phil Dawson.

"Cary Williams was the difference in the game with an inter-

Ring of Honor inductee Jamal Lewis, a former star running back, greets Ray Lewis, his former teammate, before the start of the game. *Gene Sweeney Jr. | Baltimore Sun Photo*

ception for a touchdown," Ravens coach John Harbaugh said. "Here's a guy that was under a lot of heat from [the media]. But he wasn't under heat in our building because we know what kind of player he is, and he came up big. I think he deserved that."

Weeden, who threw for 320 yards, got the ball back at his 10 with just over a minute to go and drove the Browns all the way down to the Ravens 18 after a personal foul on Paul Kruger prolonged the final drive. However, the rookie's final pass sailed out of the end zone as time expired, securing the Ravens' win.

Even with the presence of the

Morgan Cox tackles Browns punt returner Joshua Cribbs, whose helmet goes flying. Cribbs suffered a concussion after the hit by Cox and Dannell Ellerbe, not pictured. *Karl Merton Ferron | Baltimore Sun Photo*

regular officials, who debuted Thursday night after settling their differences with the league late Wednesday night, the game wasn't pretty. The Ravens had 11 penalties for 100 yards, they committed a turnover in the red zone, and rookie Justin Tucker suffered his first missed field-goal try.

However, the Ravens will head into a rare weekend off with a satisfying 3-1 record, two close victories in a five-day span, and a nine-game winning streak against the Browns.

"This is the AFC North," Harbaugh said. "This is the way it goes. It seems like every time we play those guys, this is how it goes. It's tough to win in this league. Sometimes you are going to win and you are going to look great doing it in one phase, two phases or all three phases. Sometimes, you're going to win and it's not going to look great but you have to find a way to win anyway. That's what our guys did."

Flacco was 28-for-46 for 356 yards with one touchdown to Torrey Smith, one rushing touchdown and one interception. Wide receiver Anquan Boldin caught nine passes for 139 yards with all but one of the catches coming in the second half.

Holding an uncomfortable two-point lead at halftime, the Ravens came out on their first drive of the second half and went 89 yards on 13 plays. The drive mostly belonged to Flacco and Boldin. The veteran wide receiver had an 18-yard reception on second-and-5 and then a 21-yard catch on third-and-7.

A 21-yard reception by Boldin set up the Ravens with first-and-goal. On third down from the 2, Flacco rolled out, juked a defender and went into the end zone untouched to give the Ravens a 16-7 lead with 9:53 to play.

The Browns answered with a 51-yard field goal by veteran Phil Dawson to make it a six-point game. It stayed that way as Tucker was wide right from 47 yards, his first miss of the season.

However, Williams stepped in front of Weeden's pass on the next Browns

A host of Ravens, including defensive tackle Haloti Ngata on the bottom, bring down Browns rookie running back Trent Richardson during the second quarter. *Lloyd Fox | Baltimore Sun Photo*

Referee Gene Steratore gives the thumbs-up as he walks onto the field at M&T Bank Stadium. This marked the first NFL game the league's regular officials worked since reaching an agreement to end the lockout. *Kenneth K. Lam | Baltimore Sun Photo*

drive to give the Ravens a 13-point lead.

The Ravens offense got off to a sluggish start for the second straight week only to find some rhythm in the second quarter. The unit's best opportunity in the first quarter came after Dannell Ellerbe drilled punt returner Joshua Cribbs, knocking the ball loose and his helmet off. Cribbs suffered a concussion and did not return.

The fumble gave the Ravens the ball at the Browns 40. The Ravens got it down to the Cleveland 10 thanks to three straight completions: 9 yards to Rice, 12 to Smith and 7 to Rice. However, on second down, Flacco, looking to hit Anquan Boldin in the end zone, threw into double coverage and was intercepted by Craig Robertson.

On the Ravens' next drive, Flacco made amends. On third-and-17 from his 18, Flacco lofted a nice pass to second-year receiver Tandon Doss, who ran under it for a 39-yard gain.

The next play, Flacco hit Smith down the right sideline for 34 yards.

The combination connected again, this time with Flacco finding a seam in the defense and hitting Smith in stride for an 18-yard touchdown. Flacco was 4-for-4 for 87 yards on the drive. For Smith, who lost his younger brother in a motorcycle accident the night before the Ravens' victory over the New England Patriots on Sunday, it was his third touchdown in the past two games.

Holder Sam Koch couldn't handle Morgan Cox's snap on the point after, keeping the Ravens' lead at 6-0 at 12:57 of the second quarter.

Tucker would get his shot to kick on the Ravens' next drive, and his 40-yard field-goal attempt was good, expanding the home team's lead to 9-0 and making him 7-for-7.

The Ravens appeared to be on their way to a rout as linebacker Kruger sacked Weeden to end the ensuing Browns possession.

However, Browns defensive tackle Ahtyba Rubin sacked Flacco on third down to get his team the ball back. Weeden, who was under duress for much of the first half, started the drive at his 6. He hit tight end Benjamin Watson for 6 yards on third-and-4 to give the Browns their first down of the second quarter.■

Cornerback Cary Williams returns this third-quarter interception 63 yards for a touchdown, putting the Ravens up 23-10.
Lloyd Fox | Baltimore Sun Photo

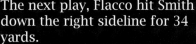

MIKE PRESTON'S REPORT CARD

QUARTERBACK — C-
Joe Flacco gets sloppy at times, and he almost got picked several times. He had opportunities to run or step up in the pocket to get more time to throw, but he didn't move well. Compared with the preseason and the regular season, this wasn't one of his better games.

RUNNING BACKS — C
The Ravens got Ray Rice into the game early but could have used him more in the third quarter. Backup Bernard Pierce ran well and almost broke a long one. The Ravens should have used Rice more in the second half, especially with the steady downpour.

RECEIVERS — A
Torrey Smith delivered several explosive plays, and Anquan Boldin came up big in the second half. Boldin controlled the middle of the field on short- and mid-range passes. He is tough to control out of the slot. This group did well all night.

OFFENSIVE LINE — D+
Tackles Michael Oher and Kelechi Osemele had trouble with Cleveland's speed on the outside, and guard Ramon Harewood and center Matt Birk couldn't knock the Browns off the ball. This group took a step back after stepping up a week ago.

DEFENSIVE LINE — C+
Tackle Haloti Ngata was a force, and the Browns had no answer for him. Cleveland also had trouble with nose guard Ma'ake Kemoeatu. The Ravens have to get more consistency from tackle Terrence Cody and ends Pernell McPhee and Arthur Jones.

LINEBACKERS — C
Outside linebacker Paul Kruger might have had his best overall game as a pro. He got pressure on Browns quarterback Brandon Weeden several times. The Ravens have to attack the run inside better, but they did a good job of getting pressure with blitzes.

SECONDARY — C-
Cornerback Cary Williams returned an interception 65 yards for a touchdown, and it was a play that changed the game. But he still has problems finding the ball, and so does nickel back Jimmy Smith. Lardarius Webb covered well, but he missed a couple of tackles.

SPECIAL TEAMS — C+
Justin Tucker made one of two field-goal tries, missing a 47-yarder wide right, and the Ravens botched a snap on an extra-point attempt. The Ravens were sound in coverage for most of the night until they allowed a long punt return in the fourth quarter.

COACHING — C-
The Ravens seemed to suffer a letdown after tough games against Philadelphia and New England. On defense, the Ravens gave up too many yards to a struggling Cleveland offense, and they don't know when to slow it down on offense.

SCORING SUMMARY

2nd Quarter
2:03	Bal	TD	T. Smith 18 pass from Flacco (kick aborted)
4:57	Bal	FG	Tucker 45
12:28	Cle	TD	Richardson 1 run (Dawson kick)

3rd Quarter
5:07	Bal	TD	Flacco 1 run (Tucker kick)
8:08	Cle	FG	Dawson 51
14:45	Bal	TD	C. Williams 63 int. return (Tucker kick)

4th Quarter
2:49	Cle	FG	Dawson 50
10:27	Cle	FG	Dawson 52

OCTOBER 7, 2012	1	2	3	4	F
RAVENS	3	0	6	0	9
CHIEFS	0	3	0	3	6

EMERGING FROM THE PILE

BY JEFF ZREBIEC, THE BALTIMORE SUN

Rookie Tucker and Chiefs' gaffes help Ravens avoid type of road loss that vexed them in 2011

KANSAS CITY, Mo. — There was enough to be concerned about and so much to correct, but the Ravens left the cramped visiting team's locker room at Arrowhead Stadium on Sunday feeling great about themselves and where they sit in the AFC North.

Over the previous three hours, they did more than enough to lose a football game to the Kansas City Chiefs. In the first half, the Ravens couldn't stop the run and were pushed around at times at the line of scrimmage. Their offense couldn't sustain a drive early and then struggled to finish one late. They turned the ball over twice and gave up a couple of big plays on special teams.

But in the end, they dodged the type of deflating loss that they had endured several times last season, relying on their rookie kicker and the charity of their opponent. Three field goals by Justin Tucker and four Chiefs turnovers — three by beleaguered quarterback Matt Cassel — were the difference in an uneven 9-6 victory in front of an announced 68,803.

Tucker converted field goals

Ravens fans kept their colors flying at Arrowhead Stadium.
Bo Rader | Photo for The Baltimore Sun

from 28, 26 and 39 yards, marking the Ravens' first win without scoring a touchdown since they beat the San Francisco 49ers, 9-7, five years earlier to the day.

"I think we did what we needed to do to win the football game, and in the National Football League, that's really what's important," Ravens coach John Harbaugh said. "That's the main thing. I think we should celebrate that, and our guys did find a way to win. If you look at it ... we won four on the road [last year], and they were against teams that maybe we weren't supposed to

win against. And the ones that we lost, they were over teams that we [were] favored against, right?

"This was one of those games that we didn't win last year, and this year we did. To me, that's the important thing and that's the big thing. Playing better? Absolutely. We have to play better, no doubt."

Sunday's victory, coupled with the Cincinnati Bengals' loss to the Miami Dolphins, gives the Ravens (4-1) a little breathing room in the division, with a

Rookie running back Bernard Pierce is tackled by Chiefs safety Eric Berry after a 12-yard gain in the third quarter.
Christopher T. Assaf | Baltimore Sun Photo

home game against the Dallas Cowboys looming Sunday. The second-place Bengals are 3-2, but the Ravens beat them in the season opener.

Sunday's win also gave the Ravens their first road victory in two tries this season and in the process reversed a script that dogged them last season in road losses to the Tennessee Titans, Jacksonville Jaguars and Seattle Seahawks.

"Games like this last year, we had a hard time winning," said running back Ray Rice, who rushed 17 times for 102 yards. "But right now, with our veteran leadership, we're finding ways to win. Obviously, this one felt good. We learned from our situation."

It was Rice — with an assist from a rare run from quarterback Joe Flacco — who put this game away. Leading 9-6 after Ryan Succop's 31-yard field goal with 4:34 to play, the Ravens got the ball and never relinquished it.

On a third-and-15 from the Ravens' 15, Flacco scrambled 16 yards for the first down. With the Chiefs down to one timeout, the Ravens ran the next three plays with Rice getting 6 yards, 3 yards and then 1 yard on third-and-1 to pick up the first down and put away the Chiefs.

"That was just part of what we had to do to win the game," said Flacco, who was just 13-for-27 for 187 yards and an interception. "They're not always pretty around here, [but] we do what we have to do to win the football game. I've been saying that for a long time, whether that's throwing for 400 yards or

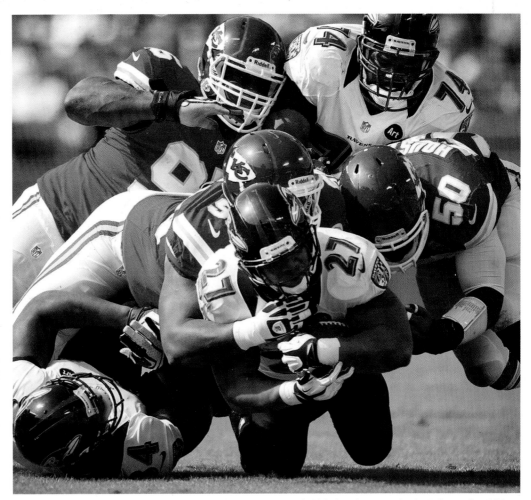

Running back Ray Rice (27) is tackled by a swarm of Chiefs. Rice carried 17 times for 102 yards. *Christopher T. Assaf | Baltimore Sun Photo*

having a [bad] day and throwing for 100 yards. We do what we have to do to win the game, and we were able to do that."

They certainly had some help, as Cassel threw two interceptions and the Chiefs (1-4) fumbled twice. But even with the help, the Ravens weren't able to shake the Chiefs until the end.

"The first half, we were flat, to be honest with you," said Ravens wide receiver Anquan Boldin, who caught four passes for 82 yards. "We hit a play here and there but would drop a ball or have a penalty to stall a drive. That's something we need to improve on."

It's fair to wonder what would have happened had the Chiefs not turned the ball over twice in a first half that ended 3-3 and was otherwise dominated by speedy running back Jamaal Charles, who had 125 of Kansas City's 179 first-half rushing yards.

The Ravens adjusted the positioning of their linebackers and defensive line, and the result was 35 rushing yards by the Chiefs in the second half, including 15 by Charles. The combination of Cassel and backup Brady Quinn combined to complete 12 of 18 passes for 124 yards and two interceptions.

It's also fair to wonder what would have happened had Cassel, who was knocked out of the game in the fourth quarter with a head injury after being hit by Haloti Ngata, not fumbled Ryan Lilja's snap on the Ravens 1-yard line while trying to score on a quarterback sneak. Ed Reed recovered the ball, and the ensuing Ravens drive resulted in a 26-

yard field goal by Tucker that gave the Ravens a 6-3 lead.

"That ended up being a 10-point swing," Harbaugh said.

It's also impossible to over-look three fourth-quarter calls that went in the Ravens' favor. On their final drive, Flacco fumbled when he was sacked by Tamba Hali. The Chiefs recovered inside the Ravens 10, but the game officials ruled that Flacco's progress had stopped before the fumble.

"I think the No. 1 thing for us coming in here was if they don't score, they don't win. That was our whole mentality," said Ravens inside linebacker Ray Lewis, who had a game-high 10 tackles but struggled to get off blocks and corral Charles in the first half. "The ones that count the most are never the pretti-est. The ones that count the most are the ones that you have to fight through. Anybody on each side of the ball will tell you that they'll take a 'W' before anything. For us to go home right now 4-1 is huge." ▪

Safety Ed Reed congratulates kicker Justin Tucker after his third field goal of the game put the Ravens up 9-3. All the game's points came on field goals. *Christopher T. Assaf | Baltimore Sun Photo*

MIKE PRESTON'S REPORT CARD

QUARTERBACK — C-
Joe Flacco had an off-day, but there were dropped passes and he was rushed often. He stared down receivers and sometimes threw late and behind them. Flacco finished with a quarterback rating of 55.6.

RUNNING BACKS — B+
Ray Rice finished with 102 rushing yards on 17 carries. He sealed the game with his running late in the fourth quarter. Fullback Vonta Leach disappears in games because of the no-huddle offense, but the Ravens make big plays when he is on the field.

RECEIVERS — C-
Anquan Boldin caught four passes for 82 yards, but the Ravens can't get open against teams that press them at the line of scrimmage. There were times receivers got open by design, but the Ravens came up with few big catches on balls that were contested.

OFFENSIVE LINE — C-
When the Ravens play against speed rushers on the outside, they might want to run more. Tackles Michael Oher and Kelechi Osemele had trouble protecting Flacco, and center Matt Birk seemed to tire as the game went on. Overall, the play was inconsistent.

DEFENSIVE LINE — C
This group played well in the second half but did a lot of arm tackling in the first half. The Ravens got decent penetration, but they didn't start getting off blocks cleanly until the second half. Even Haloti Ngata struggled in the first half.

LINEBACKERS — D
Ray Lewis led with 10 tackles, but he got pushed around. Fellow inside linebacker Jameel McClain was dominated in the first half but made improvements in the second. Outside linebacker Paul Kruger made some plays, but not enough.

SECONDARY — C+
The Ravens should have played 11 linebackers on defense because Cassel couldn't throw the ball downfield. The Ravens had two picks, but they were gifts. Safety Bernard Pollard made 10 tackles and played the run well.

SPECIAL TEAMS — C+
Justin Tucker converted all three field goals, and the Ravens did a nice job of controlling returner Javier Arenas on punt returns. But Deonte Thompson fumbled the opening kickoff of the second half, and the Ravens allowed a 41-yard kickoff return.

COACHING — C-
The Ravens seemed flat in the first half. Defensively, they made adjustments to stop the running game, but they shouldn't have taken that long. Offensively, the Ravens struggled against press coverage. They were fortunate to get the win.

SCORING SUMMARY

1st Quarter
13:39 Bal FG Tucker 28

2nd Quarter
12:12 KC FG Succop 30

3rd Quarter
7:00 Bal FG Tucker 26
15:00 Bal FG Tucker 39

4th Quarter
10:29 KC FG Succop 31

OCTOBER 14, 2012	1	2	3	4	F
COWBOYS	7	3	10	9	29
RAVENS	3	14	7	7	31

A WIN, WITH BIG LOSSES

BY JEFF ZREBIEC, THE BALTIMORE SUN

Missed field goal caps 'crazy' finish, but defense suffers key injuries

In the frantic final two minutes, Ravens players hobbled on and off the field, some occupying roles that they had never before been asked to fill. By necessity, coordinator Dean Pees sent in defensive packages that the Ravens hadn't even practiced, all while a once-seemingly comfortable lead and the NFL's longest home winning streak hung in the balance.

The Dallas Cowboys, who had the ball most of the afternoon, had two chances in the game's final 36 seconds Sunday to beat the Ravens or, at the very least, send the game into overtime.

The first one slipped through Dez Bryant's fingers, the wide receiver failing to hold on to Tony Romo's two-point conversion pass attempt that would have tied the game. The second one, after the Cowboys' recovery of an on-side kick in Ravens territory, came off Dan Bailey's right foot and then veered wide left of the upright.

Bailey's miss from 51 yards in the waning seconds allowed the Ravens to finally exhale and celebrate a 31-29 victory in front of an announced 71,384 at M&T Bank Stadium.

Linebacker Brendon Ayanbadejo celebrates after the Cowboys' Dan Bailey misses a 51-yard field goal in the final seconds that would have won the game for the Cowboys. *Karl Merton Ferron | Baltimore Sun Photo*

Fullback Vonta Leach leaps over Cowboys cornerback Morris Claiborne in the red zone. Leach's 7-yard reception set up a fourth-quarter touchdown that put the Ravens up 31-23. *Karl Merton Ferron* | *Baltimore Sun Photo*

Jacoby Jones pulls past Cowboys kicker Dan Bailey on his way to an NFL-record-tying 108-yard kickoff return in the third quarter to put the Ravens up 23-13. *Gene Sweeney Jr. | Baltimore Sun Photo*

"It was crazy to watch it over there, but we did what we needed to. I guess maybe they didn't quite do what they had to do, but it was a crazy finish," said Ravens quarterback Joe Flacco, who threw for 234 yards and one touchdown, a 19-yard strike to Torrey Smith that sent the home team into halftime with a 17-10 lead. "I don't know if we necessarily deserve to win this game, but we'll take it."

The Ravens, 5-1 for only the second time in franchise history, have a two-game lead in the AFC North and a 14-game home winning streak. Their latest victory, however, came at quite a cost, and not just to the psyche of a proud defense that continues to get pushed around at the line of scrimmage and give up yards at a staggering rate.

Lardarius Webb, the Ravens' best cornerback, likely tore the anterior cruciate ligament in his left knee late in the first quarter and could be out the rest of this season. Inside linebacker Ray Lewis, the team's leading tackler

and emotional leader, watched the Cowboys' final two drives on the sideline while getting treatment on his right arm. Lewis wasn't available to reporters after the game, but he's planning to have an MRI today on his right triceps, with the worst-case scenario being a potentially season-ending tear.

Defensive tackle Haloti Ngata, cornerback Jimmy Smith, linebacker Dannell Ellerbe and nose tackle Ma'ake Kemoeatu were also on and off the field in the second half with injuries. That forced players such as cornerback Chykie Brown and inside linebacker Brendon Ayanbadejo, who normally play on special teams, into regular duty during the Cowboys' final two drives.

"Our guys stepped up in the face of some real adversity," Ravens coach John Harbaugh said. "We had some injuries, especially on the defensive side. We were in a physical fistfight from beginning to end. They threw a lot of haymakers at us, and our guys stepped up at the end and found a way to win."

They did so despite nearly squandering leads of 24-13 and 31-23 after Ray Rice's second 1-yard touchdown run of the game with 4:41 to play.

They did so despite losing the time-of-possession battle by an astonishing 40:03-to-19:57 margin, being outgained 481-316 yards and giving up a franchise-record 227 yards on the ground to a team that was down to its third and fourth running backs by game's end. The Ravens have surrendered back-to-back 200-yard games on the ground for the first time in franchise history.

With the Ravens struggling to pressure Romo, applying very little resistance to the Cowboys' rejuvenated running game and the offense having the ball for just over a minute in the third quarter, it was Jacoby Jones who might have provided the biggest play of the game.

Returning kicks for the first time this season, Jones caught one 8 yards deep in the end zone and sprinted virtually untouched

Wide receiver Torrey Smith catches a 19-yard touchdown pass from Joe Flacco to give the Ravens a 17-10 lead in the second quarter. *Lloyd Fox | Baltimore Sun Photo*

along the right sideline. The 108-yard return gave the Ravens a 24-13 lead, tied an NFL record and set a franchise mark.

"Honestly, in practice we had one that hit the same way, so I already had a vision," Jones said. "So when I caught it, I found Anthony Allen, and he said, 'Follow me.' He was my eyes, he led me to daylight. That thing spread like the Red Sea."

While Jones' return created some separation, it did not put away the Cowboys (2-3). Romo (25-for-36 for 261 yards, two touchdowns and one interception) led an 80-yard drive that ended with a 7-yard touchdown catch by Bryant, cutting the Ravens' lead to 24-20. The drive featured runs on nine of 14 plays.

The Cowboys continued to gash the Ravens' run defense on their first possession of the fourth quarter, running on six of eight plays to set up Bailey's 34-yard field goal that trimmed the Ravens' lead to 24-23.

"I'm the one who's going to give it to you straight. For us, we have to get better," safety Bernard Pollard said. "On the defensive side of the ball, we missed tackles, starting with me. ... Our team is very talented,

our defense is very talented, but missed assignments and missed tackles are putting us in the position where it's a dogfight every game."

In five of the Ravens' six games, the outcome has been decided on the final drive. After Rice's 1-yard touchdown run Sunday made it an eight-point game, the Cowboys had a fourth-and-10, a third-and-27 and another fourth-and-10, and extended the drive long enough for Romo to hit Bryant from 4 yards out for a touchdown. When Bryant couldn't hang on to the potential game-tying 2-point conversion attempt with 32 seconds to go, it appeared the Ravens would hang on.

However, Bailey's onside kick rolled through Ayanbadejo's hands and legs, and was recovered by Andre Holmes. A pass interference call on Brown put the ball at the Ravens 34, but the Cowboys managed just 1 more yard before calling on Bailey. His kick looked good initially before veering wide left.

"The fans certainly got their money's worth today," Ravens center Matt Birk said. "It's never over until it's over. We understand that." ∎

OCTOBER 21, 2012	1	2	3	4	F
RAVENS	3	0	7	3	13
TEXANS	9	20	7	7	43

'TOSSED OUT OF THE BAR'

BY JEFF ZREBIEC, THE BALTIMORE SUN

After worst loss under Harbaugh, Ravens enter bye week with many questions

HOUSTON — The reality smacked the Ravens in the face, like one of Joe Flacco's passes that got batted back toward the line of scrimmage by a swarming Houston Texans defense.

During 60 frustrating minutes Sunday, all the Ravens' flaws through the first six games came to the surface. Flacco struggled, Ray Rice's running game never got established and the Ravens' offense wilted again on the road. On defense, not even the successful return of linebacker Terrell Suggs could save a group that struggles to tackle, get pressure on the quarterback and provide adequate coverage.

A motivated Texans team turned the showdown between the AFC's only two winning teams into a 43-13 beatdown of the Ravens in front of an announced 71,708, the biggest crowd ever at Reliant Stadium.

The most lopsided loss of the John Harbaugh era sends the Ravens (5-2) limping into the bye week with many questions about where they go from here.

"There's no sugarcoating it. Call a spade a spade. They

Nose tackle Terrence Cody (62) and coach John Harbaugh check out a video replay after the Ravens were called for a penalty in the second quarter.
Karl Merton Ferron | Baltimore Sun Photo

whipped our [butt]," said Suggs, who had four tackles and a sack just 5 1/2 months after surgery to repair a torn right Achilles tendon.

If only the Ravens' issues were that easy to diagnose and correct — or that simple. Aside from Suggs' performance, remarkable under the circumstances, a couple of nice kickoff returns from Jacoby Jones and two long field goals by rookie Justin Tucker, there were no positives for the Ravens to take away from their afternoon in the Lone Star State.

They were outgained in total yards 420-176. They lost the time-of-possession battle 38:16-21:44. Flacco completed just 21 of 43 passes, threw two interceptions, including one that was returned for a touchdown, and finished with a 45.4 quarterback rating.

Rice carried the ball just nine times and had only 54 yards of total offense. His counterpart, Arian Foster, had little trouble gouging the Ravens defense for 98 yards and two touchdowns on the ground, while Houston quarterback Matt Schaub threw for 256 yards and two touchdowns.

"Hell yeah, it's embarrassing," said inside linebacker Dannell Ellerbe, who started in place of the injured Ray Lewis. Neither Ellerbe nor cornerback Jimmy Smith, who replaced an injured Lardarius Webb, fared particularly well. "We gave up 40-some points. It seemed like everything was going in their favor today."

Linebacker Terrell Suggs played in his first game of the season after recovering from a torn Achilles tendon. He had four tackles and a sack. *Karl Merton Ferron | Baltimore Sun Photo*

After taking a 3-0 lead on their first drive, the Ravens were outscored 29-0 for the rest of the first half and outgained 413-131 the rest of the game. Nine of those points were delivered by the Texans defense: Connor Barwin came in untouched and sacked Flacco in the end zone for a safety, and Johnathan Joseph caught a ball deflected by J.J. Watt and returned it 52 yards for a touchdown.

Joseph's touchdown made the score 16-3, and the rout was on from there. In beating the Ravens for the first time in seven all-time tries, the Texans set a franchise high in points. The Ravens, meanwhile, allowed the most points since surrendering 44 to the Indianapolis Colts in December 2007.

"I'm concerned about everything," Harbaugh said. "You can talk about pretty much everything today. What aren't you concerned about? Sometimes you get tossed out of the bar. We came in with hype, with good intentions and ready to do battle. I thought our guys fought. We kept running back in, and they kept throwing us back out. ... We'll have to regroup and play a lot better in the future."

The good news is that the banged-up Ravens have a bye next weekend, giving Harbaugh and his staff more time to figure out to how to rectify the team's myriad problems that have been masked at times because of their ability to pull out games in the fourth quarter.

The first order of business will undoubtedly be attempting to fix a defense that continues to offer little resistance. After looking stout on the first three Texans drives, the Ravens allowed points on six of Houston's next eight. When Foster or Ben Tate wasn't finding holes, Andre Johnson, Owen Daniels and Kevin Walter were running free in the secondary.

Quarterback Joe Flacco grimaces as he's hit by Texans defensive end J.J. Watt while running for a first down in the third quarter. *Karl Merton Ferron | Baltimore Sun Photo*

"It's like we're two different teams on the road and at home — we can't be that," Ravens safety Ed Reed said. "We can't come here and make mistakes like we made and expect to be in the game."

While the defense has been pretty consistent with its struggles, the offense has been erratic. In four home games this year — all victories — the Ravens have totaled 129 points (32 per game) and averaged 422 total yards (314 passing and 108 running) per game while turning the ball over just twice.

In three road games — two of them losses — the Ravens have scored 45 total points (15 per game) and averaged 266 yards per game (166 passing, 100 rushing) while committing six turnovers.

Linebacker Courtney Upshaw (91) leaps over linebacker Dannell Ellerbe in pursuit of Texans running back Arian Foster, who gains 14 yards in the second quarter. Foster finished with 98 yards on 19 carries. *Karl Merton Ferron | Baltimore Sun Photo*

MIKE PRESTON'S REPORT CARD

QUARTERBACK — F
Joe Flacco had a poor day and was off the entire game. He constantly overthrew and underthrew receivers, even on short passes. He failed to get rid of the ball quickly. No quarterback should have a rating of 4.2 at halftime and 45.4 for the game.

RUNNING BACKS — C
Do the Ravens have running backs? Is Ray Rice still on the roster? It probably wouldn't have changed the course of the game, but the Ravens got away from the run too early. Rice finished with nine carries for 42 yards and five receptions for 12 yards.

RECEIVERS — C-
Either the Ravens' game plan was to throw short passes or the Texans forced them to throw short because of the pressure. Torrey Smith, the team's big-play receiver, had few chances to make plays, and only tight end Dennis Pitta was a real weapon in the game.

OFFENSIVE LINE — D-
The Ravens allowed four sacks and couldn't handle the pressure outside or inside. Houston knocked down a lot of passes because the Ravens failed to chop them at the line of scrimmage. Left tackle Michael Oher had a poor game. Left guard Bobbie Williams was even worse.

DEFENSIVE LINE — F
This group started well but couldn't sustain the effort. The Ravens couldn't get off blocks and had few plays in which they made penetration. There were times when even star Haloti Ngata struggled, and he is basically playing with one arm and one leg.

LINEBACKERS — C
Pro Bowl pick Terrell Suggs made his first appearance of the year and was the best Raven on the field. He held the edge on running plays and got a sack and several pressures. Dannell Ellerbe led all tacklers with 12, but most of those were of the Ray Lewis variety — too far down the field.

SECONDARY — F
Texans quarterback Matt Schaub picked apart the Ravens for 256 passing yards. There were times the Ravens had tight coverage, but other times the cornerbacks were playing way too soft. Cornerback Jimmy Smith will be seeing double moves in his sleep.

SPECIAL TEAMS — A
Justin Tucker had field goals of 51 and 54 yards. Jacoby Jones averaged 32.7 yards on six kick returns and had a long of 47. He was the Ravens' only offense. On five punts, Sam Koch averaged 50.6 yards. The Ravens' coverage was excellent.

COACHING — D
The Ravens were outclassed in every area, from tactics to preparation. Offensive coordinator Cam Cameron gave up on the run too soon, but there was little he could do to slow Houston's pass rush. Except for the first quarter, Dean Pees' defense could not slow the Texans.

SCORING SUMMARY

1st Quarter
4:03	Bal	FG	Tucker 51
10:11	Hou	SAF	Flacco sacked in end zone by Barwin
14:30	Hou	TD	Walter 25 pass from Schaub (Graham kick)

2nd Quarter
0:09	Hou	TD	Joseph 52 int. return (Graham kick)
9:02	Hou	TD	Daniels 1 pass from Schaub (Graham kick)
13:03	Hou	FG	Graham 33
14:57	Hou	FG	Graham 29

3rd Quarter
| 4:24 | Bal | TD | Doss 15 pass from Flacco (Tucker kick) |
| 12:04 | Hou | TD | Foster 1 run (Graham kick) |

4th Quarter
| 2:37 | Bal | FG | Tucker 54 |
| 6:12 | Hou | TD | Foster 2 run (Graham kick) |

"I don't have an explanation for it," said wide receiver Torrey Smith, who had four catches for 41 yards. Smith and Anquan Boldin were targeted 21 total times and finished with seven catches. "If I did, we'd fix it. I don't know. We're calling the same stuff, running the same stuff. But for whatever reason, we haven't been executing on the road well."

Flacco has been particularly poor on the road. At home this season, he's completed 94 of 140 passes (67.1 percent) for 1,271 yards, seven touchdowns and two interceptions.

On the road, he's 56-for-112 (50 percent) for 566 yards, two touchdowns and four interceptions.

Flacco's 15-yard pass to Tandon Doss early in the third quarter was Doss' first career touchdown and gave the Ravens offense its first score on the road in 132 minutes, 56 seconds. It was also just about all the offense accomplished Sunday.

At halftime, Flacco, who repeatedly saw balls batted back into his face, had completed just seven of 20 passes for 52 yards and two interceptions, good for a quarterback rating of 4.2. Things got a little better from there, but not by much.

"They played well, we didn't," Flacco said. "They are a good defense. They play physical, they play fast, and we just weren't able to stand up to it today and give it a good fight."∎

NOVEMBER 4, 2012	1	2	3	4	F
RAVENS	14	0	0	11	25
BROWNS	0	9	3	3	15

NOTHING FANCY ABOUT IT

BY JEFF ZREBIEC, THE BALTIMORE SUN

Ravens offense sags in middle but comes through in end with help from 'D'

CLEVELAND — During a third quarter in which the Ravens not only didn't get a first down, but also didn't net a single yard, Ravens outside linebacker Terrell Suggs sauntered over to a frustrated offense on the sidelines and delivered a message.

"We'll hold them from scoring touchdowns — you guys go ahead and pull a drive together and let's win this game," Suggs told the beleaguered group.

At the time, Suggs' comment seemed like wishful thinking. The Ravens were in the process of going 30 minutes without a first down and punting on seven straight possessions. Quarterback Joe Flacco was in the midst of misfiring on eight of nine passes. Running back Ray Rice, who gained 58 yards and scored a touchdown on 11 first-quarter carries, was immersed in a stretch of seven carries for 10 total yards.

And because of those things, their 14-point lead was gone. But as they normally do against the Cleveland Browns, the Ravens responded just in time. Flacco hit Torrey Smith for a go-ahead 19-yard touchdown with 4:26 to

Running back Ray Rice celebrates his 8-yard touchdown run with wide receiver Anquan Boldin, left, and right tackle Kelechi Osemele, right. The play put the Ravens up 7-0 in the first quarter. *Kenneth K. Lam | Baltimore Sun Photo*

play, and the Ravens defense did the rest in a 25-15 victory Sunday in front of an announced 65,449 at Cleveland Browns Stadium.

"We all knew what was happening. We all felt a change. You all felt it," said Rice, who rushed 25 times for 98 yards and a touchdown. "But we also knew that when our defense was stopping them, when

they were only kicking field goals, that we had a chance to win this game. We had no doubt that we were going to go out there and put a drive together to come out ahead.

"As far as Ravens football, we've never been a fancy group. We've never been a group that wins, quite frankly, pretty.

Defensive end Arthur Jones (97) and linebacker Dannell Ellerbe (59) take down Browns rookie running back Trent Richardson in the second quarter. Richardson rushed 25 times for 105 yards. *Kenneth K. Lam | Baltimore Sun Photo*

When you're 6-2, there's just no complaining about it."

Whether the spark came on Smith's catch and spin past Joe Haden on his way to the end zone, or on Anquan Boldin's clutch 21-yard catch earlier in the drive to break a long first-down drought, it was needed nonetheless. The win's immedi-

ate impact was evident throughout a relieved locker room.

The Ravens are now 6-2, including 2-2 on the road, heading into Sunday's matchup with the Oakland Raiders at M&T Bank Stadium, where the Ravens haven't lost since December 2010. The Ravens swept the season series against a divisional

foe and have now beaten the Browns (2-7) 10 straight times. They are 3-0 this season against the AFC North and have won an NFL-high 11 straight games against divisional opponents.

"We started fast and we finished strong. In the middle, we were a little like this," said Ravens coach John Harbaugh, waving his hand wildly. "It was a little iffy there, but the thing I was proud of, our guys played with faith in one another. When the offense was struggling, the defense wasn't. When the defense struggled, the offense wasn't. We came together at the end to win the game."

Two plays after Brandon Weeden completed an 18-yard touchdown to Josh Gordon that was nullified by an illegal-formation penalty, Phil Dawson kicked his fifth field goal of the day, this one from 41 yards, to give Cleveland a 15-14 lead with 8:48 to play.

When the Ravens got the ball back at their 19 with 8:44 remaining, they hadn't gotten a first down since the 8:38 mark of the second quarter. They had failed on seven consecutive third-down conversions. The wide receivers weren't getting open, and Rice had no room to run. And predictably, the first play of the drive resulted in a dropped pass by Smith.

What finally got the Ravens going was Flacco's 21-yard strike to Boldin on second-and-10 from the 19.

"We just needed one play to break the ice, and that was it," fullback Vonta Leach said.

A penalty for roughing the passer gave the Ravens the ball on the Browns 32. On third and-10 from the 19, Flacco hit Smith in the right flat and he spun past Haden and sprinted untouched to the end zone. It was the Ravens' first third-down conversion since the first quarter, when they went 4-for-4 on third downs.

"There were a few plays I felt like I could have made earlier in the game," Smith said. "I was frustrated by it, so I was glad we got to finish on the good side."

A 2-point conversion pass to Boldin made the score 22-15. The Ravens defense, which allowed 105 rushing yards to im-

After catching a pass from Joe Flacco, wide receiver Torrey Smith races toward the end zone for a 19-yard touchdown. The Ravens went up 22-15 after a 2-point conversion with 4:26 left in the game. *Kenneth K. Lam | Baltimore Sun Photo*

Browns defensive ends Juqua Parker (95) and Jabaal Sheard (97) sack Joe Flacco for an 8-yard loss during the third quarter. *Kenneth K. Lam | Baltimore Sun Photo*

QUARTERBACK — C
Joe Flacco started out strong but went cold in the second half along with the rest of the offense. Flacco threw well when he had the time but struggled to connect with Torrey Smith on deep passes.

RUNNING BACKS — C+
Ray Rice had 25 rushes for 98 yards and caught two passes for 6 yards. And the Ravens won. Surprise, surprise. Rice earned most of those yards on his own and had very little blocking in the second half.

RECEIVERS — C+
Flacco found Anquan Boldin early in the game, especially off play-action and on short- to mid-range passes. The Ravens did a nice job of finding the seams in Cleveland's zone, and Smith had a nice move after the catch on his 19-yard touchdown in the fourth quarter.

OFFENSIVE LINE — C-
This group started out strong and dominated in the first half, especially left tackle Michael Oher and left guard Bobbie Williams. But in the second half, the Browns started winning the one-on-one matchups and shut down the Ravens.

DEFENSIVE LINE — D
The Ravens didn't get a lot from this group even though it did a better job of getting penetration in the second half. Arthur Jones finished with four tackles, and tackle Terrence Cody had one. Haloti Ngata wasn't credited with a tackle.

LINEBACKERS — C+
Dannell Ellerbe appeared to have a strong game with nine tackles, but he still tackles too much with his arms instead of his body. The Ravens didn't get much out of their outside linebackers, including Terrell Suggs, but outside linebacker Courtney Upshaw played well against the run.

SECONDARY — C-
The Ravens appeared to play more zone than usual, and that surprised Browns quarterback Brandon Weeden, who acknowledged it after the game. Cornerbacks Jimmy Smith and Cary Williams lost receivers at times, and safety Ed Reed missed a lot of tackles.

SPECIAL TEAMS — B+
Justin Tucker converted a 43-yard field goal, and the Ravens did a nice job of controlling Browns return specialist Joshua Cribbs. Brendon Ayanbadejo had two tackles to lead the Ravens.

COACHING — C+
The Ravens were smart enough to commit to a run-control offense, but despite going with Rice, they had no counter to the Browns' adjustments in the second half. Defensively, the Ravens still have to find a way to get more of a pass rush.

pressive rookie Trent Richardson but forced five field goals on five trips inside their red zone, stopped Cleveland on fourth down.

Justin Tucker converted the field position into a 43-yard field goal, and Ed Reed intercepted Weeden on the Browns' final possession.

"Somebody just mentioned to me, 'Was it frustrating?' No, it wasn't frustrating at all. We knew what was happening to us. Cleveland has a good defense. I don't care what people think," Ravens offensive coordinator Cam Cameron said. "Give our guys credit for that last drive. The defense played complementary football. We got better during the bye."

Cameron had heard plenty of criticism during the week after Rice got just nine carries and rookie Bernard Pierce didn't get any in a 43-13 loss to the Houston Texans two weeks ago. The Ravens responded by rushing on 16 of their 22 offensive plays in a first quarter in which they outgained Cleveland in yards 156-22 and controlled the time of possession by a margin of 12:17 to 2:43.

An 8-yard touchdown by Rice and a 12-yard score from Pierce — the first of his pro career — gave the Ravens a 14-0 lead after the first quarter. But by halftime, it was 14-9 and the Ravens offense, which had struggled on the road all season, was again in a funk.

It took some time, as their seemingly comfortable two-touchdown lead vanished, but the Ravens woke up just in time.

"I don't take any credence in winning ugly. To me, it doesn't mean anything," Harbaugh said. "We're going to have lots to work on next week. We are going to try to become a great football team. We're not there by any stretch, [but] we have a chance to get there if we all come together and do the things we need to get there." ■

SCORING SUMMARY

1st Quarter

6:28	Bal	TD	Rice 8 run (Tucker kick)
14:59	Bal	TD	Pierce 12 run (Tucker kick)

2nd Quarter

5:41	Cle	FG	Dawson 32
13:13	Cle	FG	Dawson 28
14:57	Cle	FG	Dawson 29

3rd Quarter

12:21	Cle	FG	Dawson 33

4th Quarter

6:12	Cle	FG	Dawson 41
10:34	Bal	TD	T. Smith 19 pass from Flacco (Boldin pass from Flacco)
12:11	Bal	FG	Tucker 43

NOVEMBER 11, 2012	1	2	3	4	F
RAIDERS	0	10	7	3	20
RAVENS	10	17	21	7	55

GOOD DAY TO PILE ON

BY JEFF ZREBIEC, THE BALTIMORE SUN

Franchise marks set, all units excel as home winning streak hits 15

There was Ray Rice going untouched for a 7-yard touchdown run. Torrey Smith sprinting free behind the Oakland Raiders defense and connecting with Joe Flacco for a 47-yard score. Holder Sam Koch encountering very little resistance during his 7-yard touchdown scamper on a fake field goal.

And just when it seemed as though it couldn't get any worse for the hapless and defenseless Oakland Raiders, the Ravens' Jacoby Jones took a kickoff 5 yards deep in the end zone and both he and his lead blocker, Anthony Allen, sprinted down the right sideline with nary an opposing player in sight.

Jones' 105-yard touchdown return early in the fourth quarter capped an afternoon of record-setting dominance for the Ravens and helplessness for the Raiders. In a 55-20 beat-down in front of an announced 71,339 at M&T Bank Stadium, the Ravens set a franchise record for points and got a little swagger back in preparation for next Sunday's showdown against the second-place Pittsburgh Steelers.

The Steelers still have to face the Kansas City Chiefs tonight,

Holder Sam Koch, center, celebrates with tackles Michael Oher and Kelechi Osemele after scoring a 7-yard touchdown on a fake field goal to put the Ravens up 48-17 in the third quarter. *Kenneth K. Lam | Baltimore Sun Photo*

but the Ravens know they'll go into next week's game — the first of two matchups against their rival in a three-week span — in sole possession of first place in the AFC North.

"This is Ravens football. That was as close to 60 minutes as a team that we've played all year long," said safety Bernard Pollard,

who led a defense that forced two of the Raiders' three turnovers and sacked quarterback Carson Palmer three times. "I just really believe that we have to continue this. We have to continue to stack these weeks."

In winning for the 15th consecutive time at home and im-

proving to 7-2 for the first time in the John Harbaugh era and the second time in franchise history, the Ravens had a 10-point lead at the end of the first quarter, a 27-10 advantage at halftime and a 48-17 spread after the third quarter. The 48 points, reached when Koch ran in the fake field goal and then celebrated with an emphatic spike, tied the record for the most points in franchise history. And there were still more than 20 minutes to play.

Jones set the record about eight minutes later, when he became the first player in Ravens history to have two kickoff-return touchdowns, both for a season and for a career. He celebrated the score with a dance in the back of the end zone and might have exerted more energy on the dance than on the touchdown, because once he broke free from the initial wave, Jones wasn't touched.

"I was surprised that it got that way early, but obviously they're banged up and we wanted to come out there and try to get a win," said Rice, who had 35 rushing yards and 33 receiving yards. "But to score 55 and everybody's involved, it felt pretty good."

Shrugging off consecutive subpar performances on the road, Flacco com-

Wide receiver Torrey Smith catches a 47-yard touchdown pass in front of Raiders safety Tyvon Branch to give the Ravens a 34-10 lead early in the third quarter. *Kenneth K. Lam | Baltimore Sun Photo*

Quarterback Joe Flacco scores a touchdown on a 1-yard sneak, putting the Ravens ahead 10-0 in the first quarter.
Lloyd Fox | Baltimore Sun Photo

pleted 21 of 33 passes for 341 yards, three touchdowns and one interception before giving way to backup Tyrod Taylor early in the fourth quarter. Smith (Maryland) caught just two passes, but both went for touchdowns — the 47-yarder on just the third play of the third quarter and a 20-yarder about 4 minutes later after the Raiders fumbled a punt.

Tight end Dennis Pitta, silent the previous couple of weeks, returned as a major part of the Ravens' game plan, catching five balls for 67 yards and a touch-down.

"Obviously, we had success. We ran the game plan, and it worked well," Flacco said. "We scored points early and continued to score them."

The Ravens rolled up 419 yards of total offense, committed just one turnover and a season-low four penalties, and punted just twice in the first three quarters. Because of the big lead, the Ravens never had to play injured Pro Bowl defensive tackle Haloti Ngata (knee/shoulder) and second-year cornerback Jimmy Smith (groin), though both were active.

They also were able to rest several starters, including Rice and safety Ed Reed, who suffered a shoulder stinger on a missed tackle that led to a 55-yard touchdown catch by Darrius Heyward-Bey (McDonogh, Maryland) late in the second quarter. Palmer, who threw for 368 yards, also hit Denarius Moore for a 30-yard score early in the third.

"All three phases played exceptionally well," Harbaugh said. "I thought we started fast. We finished well and we played pretty good in between, which we haven't always done. So that's a

Raiders fullback Marcell Reece (45) is crushed by nose tackle Ma'ake Ke-moeatu (96), linebacker Jameel McClain (53) and linebacker Albert Mc-Clellan (50) during the first quarter. Oakland rushed for just 72 yards in the game. *Christopher T. Assaf | Baltimore Sun Photo*

good step in the right direction. ... To single one guy out would be probably doing a disservice to the whole team. I thought it was a great team victory."

Harbaugh praised all three of his units, specifically mentioning the way the defense batted down six passes by Palmer and citing the special teams for the two touchdowns and the one caused turnover. When the Ravens chose to fake the field goal, they had the ball at the Raiders 7 and led 41-17. Afterward, Harbaugh offered no apologies, saying the Ravens took the opportunity they were given, and Raiders first-year coach Dennis Allen didn't want one. He had too much else to be angry about after a performance that he called "unacceptable.

"It's our job to go out and stop them," he said when asked whether he was bothered by the fake field goal.

The Ravens know that they'll get much more resistance next week against a Steelers defense that entered Sunday ranked first in the NFL. At least in theory, Sunday's performance gave the Ravens momentum and provided a boost for an offense that had sputtered recently. However, a number of Ravens shot down the notion.

"I don't know if we needed it. We just need to win every week," veteran center Matt Birk said. "The most important thing is we won. We're probably not as good as the score showed today, and we understand that."

They also understand what lies ahead, a challenge cornerback Cary Williams summed up succinctly by saying: "We understand what [the Steelers are] going to bring to the table. We don't like them, they don't like us. It's going to be hell out there." ∎

NOVEMBER 18, 2012	1	2	3	4	F
RAVENS	10	0	3	0	13
STEELERS	7	0	3	0	10

BACK TO THE OLD GRIND

BY JEFF ZREBIEC, THE BALTIMORE SUN

Rivalry produces another defense-dominated contest as Ravens take 2-game lead in AFC North

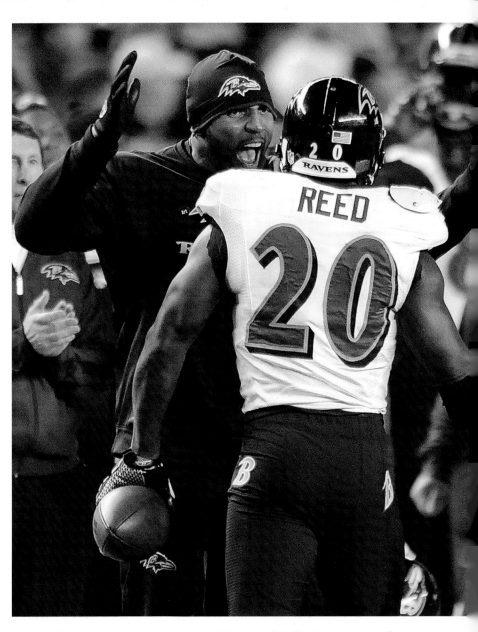

Injured linebacker Ray Lewis congratulates safety Ed Reed, whose fumble recovery and 17-yard runback set up a first-quarter field goal that pulled the Ravens within 7-3. *Lloyd Fox | Baltimore Sun Photo*

PITTSBURGH — There was no Ben Roethlisberger, Hines Ward or Ray Lewis, but as both teams predicted all week, it turned out to be more of the same from the Ravens-Pittsburgh Steelers rivalry.

In a tense game dominated by defense, the Ravens' Jacoby Jones made the game's decisive play with a 63-yard punt return for a touchdown in the first quarter. The Ravens defense did the rest in a 13-10 victory over the Byron Leftwich-led Steelers in front of an announced 63,446 at Heinz Field.

The Ravens improved to 8-2 this season and have a two-game lead in the AFC North. The Steelers fell to 6-4. The teams will play again in two weeks, but up next for the Ravens is a West Coast trip to face the San Diego Chargers on Sunday.

"It's never pretty in this game," Ravens coach John Harbaugh said. "I think it's the usual, right? Three-point spread? Isn't that what these usually are? We got a typical Pittsburgh-Baltimore game."

After allowing a touchdown in the opening minute of the game on a 31-yard scramble by Leftwich, the Ravens defense wouldn't allow the Steelers into the end zone again. Trailing 13-10, the Steelers got the ball back at their 16 with 1:05 to play and no timeouts, but they did nothing with it, and the Ravens poured onto the field to celebrate their latest victory over their division rival and third consecutive regular-season win at Heinz Field.

"It wasn't the same kind of game because [Lewis] wasn't playing, [Lardarius Webb] wasn't playing," Ravens outside linebacker Terrell Suggs said. "They had a couple of key guys out. It's bittersweet. You're glad to win, but you don't want to leave no stone unturned. You don't want them to be able to have no excuses, to be able to say, 'Oh, Ben didn't play.' But we'll take the 'W'. We'd prefer the 'W' with [Roethlisberger] under center and [Troy Polamalu] out there."

Justin Tucker points to the sky after his 39-yard field goal gave the Ravens a 13-7 lead midway through the third quarter. *Gene Sweeney Jr. | Baltimore Sun Photo*

Jacoby Jones pulls away from would-be Steelers tacklers to return a punt 63 yards for a touchdown. The play gave the Ravens a 10-7 lead late in the first quarter.   *Lloyd Fox | Baltimore Sun Photo*

Leftwich committed his first turnover on the Steelers' first drive of the third quarter. After a 37-yard completion to Emmanuel Sanders put the ball into Ravens territory, Leftwich tried to force another ball to Sanders but cornerback Corey Graham, getting the start with Webb and Jimmy Smith sidelined, stepped in front of it at the 18. He returned it all the way to the Ravens 38.

The Ravens converted the turnover into points. A 23-yard completion from Flacco to Anquan Boldin and a key 8-yard third-down catch by Ray Rice put Justin Tucker in position to hit a 39-yard field goal. That gave the Ravens a 13-7 lead with 6:49 left in the third quarter.

But the Steelers, whose offense had done nothing since

their opening drive, answered immediately. With Pittsburgh getting the ball at its 16, Leftwich hit running back Jonathan Dwyer for a 15-yard gain. The Steelers then started to get their running game going with Dwyer running for gains of 7 and 11 yards.

A 23-yard completion by Leftwich to Sanders, coupled with an unnecessary-roughness penalty on Ed Reed, who was called for a helmet-to-helmet hit, put the ball down to the Ravens 12. After an 8-yard run by Dwyer advanced the ball to the 4, Leftwich threw back-to-back incompletions to the right corner of the end zone.

Shaun Suisham then hit a 22-yard field goal to cap a 12-play, 80-yard drive and cut the Ravens' lead to 13-10 with 37 seconds to play in the third quarter.

On their next two drives, both

in the fourth quarter, the Steelers advanced into Ravens territory but a sack by Haloti Ngata forced a punt on one drive and a sack by reserve safety James Ihedigbo forced a punt on the next.

With Roethlisberger on the sideline with his right arm in a sling, Leftwich was making his first start since 2009. The Steelers talked all week about tailoring their offense to suit the veteran's skill set.

Sure enough, on the Steelers' first play from scrimmage, Leftwich threw the ball deep down to the left sideline to speedy wide receiver Mike Wallace. The pass fell incomplete, but Ravens cornerback Cary Williams was called for pass interference, a 42-yard penalty.

Two plays later, Leftwich rolled out to his right, outrunning Suggs to get out of the pocket. He then

Corey Graham returns an interception of a deep pass by Steelers quarterback Byron Leftwich in the third quarter. The pick set up Justin Tucker's 39-yard field goal. *Gene Sweeney Jr. | Baltimore Sun Photo*

QUARTERBACK — C-
Joe Flacco's numbers don't look bad, but most of his yardage came on short passes. He often threw high and became erratic in the pocket when pressured.

RUNNING BACKS — C+
Ray Rice ran hard, but there were few holes and the Steelers closed off the cutback lanes. Rookie running back Bernard Pierce played well during his limited time on the field.

RECEIVERS — C-
The only one who could get open frequently was Anquan Boldin, and the Steelers gave him a lot of cushion at the line of scrimmage. Second-year player Torrey Smith had just one catch. He might have done too many interviews last week.

OFFENSIVE LINE — D
Center Matt Birk and left guard Jah Reid got handled up front. The Ravens did an adequate job of pass blocking, but there were no open lanes to run the ball.

DEFENSIVE LINE — B
This might have been this group's best game. Tackle Arthur Jones made a couple of plays, and the Steelers had no answer for tackle Haloti Ngata. The Ravens even collapsed the pocket a couple of times.

LINEBACKERS — B
Outside linebacker Paul Kruger might have had his best game in a Ravens uniform, and he kept constant pressure on quarterback Byron Leftwich. The Ravens also did a good job of holding the edge on most running plays. Inside linebacker Dannell Ellerbe had a strong game.

SECONDARY — B
The Ravens got off to a slow start but for the most part held their own and positioned themselves well. For a group that has been ravaged by injuries, it was an impressive performance.

SPECIAL TEAMS — A-
This group continues to carry the Ravens and kept Pittsburgh pinned down most of the night. Justin Tucker missed a costly field-goal try, but Jacoby Jones had a 63-yard punt return, his third return score this season.

COACHING — B
It's tough to play on the road in Pittsburgh, but the Ravens were mentally ready. They dominated the Steelers on defense and special teams, but the offense did little except avoid costly turnovers.

broke through an arm tackle by safety Bernard Pollard on his way down the sideline for a 31-yard touchdown. It was the longest scoring run of his career.

"We said he was a statue," Suggs said. "We said that he wasn't going to move and he proved all of us wrong."

The Ravens went three-and-out on their first possession and lost one of their top playmakers in the process. Tight end Dennis Pitta, who was hit by Lawrence Timmons and Ryan Clark while making a 5-yard catch on third down, suffered a concussion and didn't return to the game.

But trailing 7-0, the Ravens got a big lift from one of their newest defensive players. On third-and-10, Leftwich hit Wallace on a slant but cornerback Chris Johnson, who was playing in his first game this season, stripped Wallace of the ball. Safety Ed Reed recovered it at the Steelers 29 and ran it all the way to the 12-yard line.

The Ravens were forced to settle for a 26-yard field goal by rookie Justin Tucker to put

them on the board. They'd get into the end zone about five minutes later, but it would happen with their offense on the sideline.

Jones, whom the Ravens acquired this offseason to provide big plays in big games just like this, fielded a 51-yard punt from rookie Drew Butler at the Ravens 37. He cut toward the left sideline and then cut back up the field, where he found plenty of open grass. The last man to beat was Butler and Jones did that with relative ease to finish off a 63-yard touchdown run.

"It's a Ravens-Steelers game. ... We expected this to be a net punting-type game and a significant play was going to swing it," Steelers coach Mike Tomlin said. "Unfortunately for us, they provided a significant play with the punt return."

Jones' touchdown, which he culminated with an elaborate dance in the corner of the end zone, gave the Ravens a 10-7 lead and was his third return touchdown this season. No Raven had ever done that.▪

SCORING SUMMARY

1st Quarter
0:43	Pit	TD	Leftwich 31 run (Suisham kick)
6:38	Bal	FG	Tucker 26
11:44	Bal	TD	J. Jones 63 punt return (Tucker kick)

3rd Quarter
8:11	Bal	FG	Tucker 39
14:26	Pit	FG	Suisham 22

NOVEMBER 25, 2012	1	2	3	4	OT	F
RAVENS	0	0	3	10	3	16
CHARGERS	0	10	0	3	0	13

4TH-AND-29 PLAY SAVES DAY

BY JEFF ZREBIEC, THE BALTIMORE SUN

'Rice up the middle' sets up tying field goal by Tucker, who kicks winner in overtime

SAN DIEGO — When Ray Rice caught the ball and looked upfield, his challenge — and the Ravens' chances of pulling out a victory over the San Diego Chargers — seemed pretty close to hopeless.

There were defenders rushing toward Rice and about 20 yards he still needed to cover to get a first down. Running down the sideline, Rice made two defenders miss and then outran a couple more as he cut across the field. He contemplated taking it all the way to the opposite sideline before ultimately deciding to keep inching forward.

When his mad dash was finally over and Rice was knocked down at the Chargers 34-yard line, the Ravens had their first down. And about 45 minutes later, they had a victory that looked improbable for much of the afternoon. Rice's 29-yard catch-and-run on fourth-and-29 set up Justin Tucker's game-tying 38-yard field goal as time expired in regulation.

Tucker then hit from 38 yards with 1:07 remaining in overtime Sunday as the Ravens fought back from 10 points down with less than 8 minutes to go to defeat the

Coach John Harbaugh high-fives fans after the Ravens' unlikely victory at Qualcomm Stadium gave them a 9-2 record and three-game lead in the AFC North. *Kenneth K. Lam | Baltimore Sun Photo*

Chargers, 16-13, in front of an announced 57,822 at Qualcomm Stadium.

"We have a football team that has the biggest hearts that I've ever seen. I don't want to go overboard here, but how can you not?" Ravens coach John Harbaugh said. "Have you ever been part of a game like that? Have you ever seen a game

like that? I never have."

With the victory, the Ravens improved to 9-2 and took a three-game lead in the AFC North over the Pittsburgh Steelers and the Cincinnati Bengals. The Steelers, who lost earlier in the day to the last-place Cleveland Browns, will be in Baltimore on Sunday and a Ravens

Running back Ray Rice wills his way downfield for 29 yards on a fourth-and-29 dump-off pass from Joe Flacco. The miraculous play helped set up Justin Tucker's tying field goal at the end of regulation.
Karl Merton Ferron | Baltimore Sun Photo

victory would go a long way toward sewing up the division.

While several Ravens stopped short of declaring the victory a potential season-defining moment, all of them agreed they had never seen anything quite like Rice's play, which came on a dump-off after quarterback Joe Flacco decided against just throwing the ball up for grabs from his 37 with 1:59 to play in the fourth quarter.

"It was really kind of a Hail Mary situation," Flacco said. "We were running down the field and I was hoping because they were playing so soft, sometimes you can kind of get in behind one of those guys and catch them flat-footed and maybe find a soft spot and rip a ball real quick into somebody. I didn't really see anything like that. I didn't want to just throw a Hail Mary. I wanted to give somebody a chance."

Linebacker Terrell Suggs sacks the Chargers' Philip Rivers for a 7-yard loss on second-and-10 from the Ravens 22 in the second quarter. San Diego had to settle for a field goal. *Kenneth K. Lam | Baltimore Sun Photo*

Rice wasn't sure how good a chance he had, but once he broke the first tackle down the right sideline, he started to sense that things were opening up.

"On that play, it was just will, man," Rice said. "It was just a simple call. There are not too many calls you can [make] on that play. They dropped in max coverage. I guess they figured if they are dropping it down to the guy, they make the tackle and game over. I guess when you put me into the equation, I guess it's not that easy."

Referee Gene Steratore presided over a lengthy review of the play and ultimately moved the ball back a yard and reset the yard markers. But the measurement confirmed that the Ravens had gotten the first down. Six plays later, Tucker kicked the ball through the uprights to send the game into overtime.

Rice nicknamed his decisive play, "Hey diddle diddle, Rice up the middle." Both wide receiver Torrey Smith (Maryland) and defensive tackle Haloti Ngata called it the best play that they'd ever seen.

Linebacker Terrell Suggs, meanwhile, couldn't believe that Rice not only got the ball, but also kept it.

"I was thinking we needed a miracle," Suggs said. "I was thinking we have Jacoby Jones and he can jump there and catch it or we have Anquan Boldin with the best hands in the world. But then I saw the check-down to Ray Rice and I thought he was going to pitch it or something but he kept it and made an amazing play to get it done for us."

The Ravens then had to sweat

Justin Tucker, right, celebrates with holder Sam Koch after kicking the winning 38-yard field goal with 1:07 left in overtime.   *Kenneth K. Lam | Baltimore Sun Photo*

MIKE PRESTON'S REPORT CARD

QUARTERBACK — B+
Joe Flacco started off slowly, and it appeared he would have another poor performance on the road. But he played well in the second half and made some big-time throws late in the fourth quarter and in overtime. The pass to Torrey Smith to set up the game-winning field goal was a beauty.

RUNNING BACKS — A
Ray Rice finished with 97 yards on 22 carries and had eight catches for 67 yards. His run after a short pass on fourth-and-29 in the fourth quarter was an amazing display of speed, power, burst and balance.

RECEIVERS — B
Once the Ravens started going up-tempo with the offense, San Diego had no one to contain the receivers. Smith was too much for the Chargers to handle on the outside, and San Diego couldn't control Anquan Boldin in the slot or tight end Dennis Pitta over the middle.

OFFENSIVE LINE — C
This group, especially offensive tackle Kelechi Osemele, struggled with the Chargers pass rush early in the game. But the Ravens kept San Diego in check when the game was on the line. The Chargers had five sacks.

DEFENSIVE LINE — B+
San Diego had 91 rushing yards, but it was a quiet 91 yards. Tackles Ma'ake Kemoeatu and Haloti Ngata did a good job of plugging the middle, and end-tackle Arthur Jones played a good game for the second week in a row.

LINEBACKERS — B+
Outside linebackers Paul Kruger and Terrell Suggs provided a lot of pressure as the Ravens finished with six sacks. Inside linebacker Jameel McClain had several big hits when stopping the run, and reserve Brendon Ayanbadejo was superb in pass coverage filling in for the injured Dannell Ellerbe.

SECONDARY — B+
San Diego had 228 passing yards, but the Ravens did a nice job with coverage, especially in the second half. A couple of the sacks were because cornerbacks Cary Williams and Corey Graham had tight coverage. This group had some lapses early in the game but recovered well.

SPECIAL TEAMS — B
It's rare, but it was not a strong day punting for Sam Koch. Rookie Justin Tucker converted on three field goals, including the game-winner from 38 yards. The Ravens covered well, but returner Jacoby Jones should gamble less with some punt returns.

COACHING — B
Coach John Harbaugh was in a tough spot having to travel to the West Coast between games against Pittsburgh. After a sluggish first half, the offense warmed up and got going in the second half. The defense played well throughout.

out a few more anxious moments in overtime, but their defense, which sacked the Chargers' Philip Rivers a season-high six times and was stingy after Malcom Floyd's 21-yard touchdown catch early in the second quarter, forced punts on both of San Diego's overtime possessions.

The Ravens punted on their first possession of overtime as well. On their second, they got the ball at their 11. Flacco moved the chains on the strength of completions to Dennis Pitta and Tandon Doss before he connected with Smith (seven catches for 144 yards) on a beautiful 31-yard strike down the right sideline to get the ball to the Chargers 16.

After three kneel-downs to center the ball and get the overtime clock down near one minute, Tucker came on and delivered from 38 yards to end it.

"When it comes down to it, this is a job and you just got to do it," Tucker said. "Morgan [Cox] threw back two great snaps, Sam [Koch] gave me two great holds and that makes my job pretty [darn] easy."

Little came easy for the Ravens on this day. They trailed 13-3 with under 8 minutes to go, and it had been about an 8 1/2 quarters since they had scored an offensive touchdown.

However, Flacco took the Ravens 80 yards and hit Pitta for a 4-yard touchdown to make it a 13-10 game. The Ravens defense then forced another three-and-out to set the stage for Rice's heroics.

"I don't think it was a good shot, but I thought our best shot was to just kind of give it to Ray. Ray made a great run, we got a little lucky. It worked out perfect," Flacco said. "I said to somebody, we played 55 minutes of pretty ugly football but this team knows how to win and that's what you saw today."∎

SCORING SUMMARY

2nd Quarter
5:17   SD   TD   Floyd 21 pass from Rivers (Novak kick)
11:56 SD   FG   Novak 47

3rd Quarter
2:41   Bal FG   Tucker 43

4th Quarter
7:09   SD   FG   Novak 30
10:41 Bal TD   Pitta 4 pass from Flacco (Tucker kick)
15:00 Bal FG   Tucker 38

Overtime
13:53 Bal FG   Tucker 38

DECEMBER 2, 2012	1	2	3	4	F
STEELERS	3	3	7	10	23
RAVENS	0	13	7	0	20

AN OPPORTUNITY SQUANDERED

BY JEFF ZREBIEC, THE BALTIMORE SUN

Ravens fail to clinch playoff spot as backup Batch rallies Steelers in fourth quarter

It wasn't simply the disgust of watching the Pittsburgh Steelers, their most hated rival, come to their stadium and revive their own season while temporarily delaying the Ravens' bid to clinch a playoff spot.

That surely hurt, but it was the manner in which it happened and what it means going forward that left the Ravens quietly trudging out of their locker room Sunday night, some shell-shocked and searching for answers, others proclaiming that they had just beaten themselves.

In a season in which the Ravens have consistently found ways to win, regardless of how much they struggled and how bleak things looked, they discovered a deflating way to lose. They allowed Charlie Batch, a third-string, soon-to-be 38-year-old quarterback, to dig his team out of a fourth-quarter deficit and drive it down the field in the final minutes to set up the game-winning score.

Shaun Suisham's 42-yard field goal as time expired sent the Steelers to a 23-20 victory in front of an announced 71,442 — the second-largest crowd at M&T Bank Stadium history — and left the Ravens in a significantly less desirable position than they had been when the day began.

"It [stinks] to let this one go," Ravens safety Bernard Pollard said. "Right now we're just trying to figure out how and why. Right now we're eating humble pie, and nobody likes to do that. This is a win

Quarterback Joe Flacco rips off his helmet in frustration after the Ravens failed to convert on third down. They settled for one of Justin Tucker's two second-quarter field goals. *Lloyd Fox | Baltimore Sun Photo*

Six Ravens, including linebacker Terrell Suggs, gang-tackle Steelers running back Isaac Redman during the third quarter. Redman, a Bowie State alumnus, carried nine times for 43 yards. *Lloyd Fox* | *Baltimore Sun Photo*

that we should have had. You can say whatever you want to say, but for us, this [stinks]. It [stinks] to let a team off the hook. It's something we have to deal with until we play next week."

Ravens coach John Harbaugh was quick to say that the loss would not "define" his team's season, but it certainly could have significant ramifications, including the potential loss of Pro Bowl outside linebacker Terrell Suggs, who was forced from the game with an arm injury and will be evaluated in the days ahead.

The Ravens (9-3) were immediately left to digest the end of their 16-game home winning streak (which includes the playoffs) and their 12-game divisional winning streak. Before Sunday, the Steelers also had the previous win by an opponent at M&T Bank Stadium, and that came in December 2010.

After starting the day with a chance to clinch a playoff berth with a win and secure the division title with a victory and a Cincinnati Bengals loss to the San Diego Chargers, the Ravens watched their divisional lead shrink to two games over the Steelers and Bengals, who also won. The Ravens also fell into the No. 3 playoff slot in the AFC.

The Ravens, New England Patriots and Denver Broncos are tied with 9-3 records; even though the Patriots lost to the Ravens in Week 3, New England has a better conference record (8-1) than the Ravens (8-2) and the Broncos (6-2), so it holds the No. 2 spot. The picture should become clearer when the Ravens host the Broncos in two weeks.

That's part of a difficult four-game, season-ending stretch for the Ravens, which starts Sunday in Landover against the Washington Redskins.

"We just have to regroup," said Ravens safety Ed Reed, who had an interception and a fumble recovery. "We know this is a journey. We are into the fourth quarter of this

Running back Ray Rice dashes 34 yards for a touchdown with 5 minutes left in the third quarter to put the Ravens up 20-13. Rice carried 12 times for 78 yards. *Lloyd Fox | Baltimore Sun Photo*

thing. We wanted to be 4-0 in the third quarter, but we are not. We have a tough schedule coming up. This is far from over."

Reed cited a couple of key turnovers by the offense and the defense's failure to get off the field on third down as the Ravens' biggest issues in allowing a 13-3 second-quarter lead and a 20-13 fourth-quarter advantage to be overcome by a Steelers team that was playing without starting quarterback Ben Roethlisberger for the third straight game.

Ray Rice's 34-yard touchdown run, which came after Steelers wide receiver Emmanuel Sanders fumbled the ball untouched despite having an open lane to the end zone, had given the Ravens a 20-13 lead with 4:50 to play in the third quarter. But after that run, the Ravens offense managed to

get only two more first downs.

"Everything is about execution," said Ravens wide receiver Torrey Smith (Maryland), who had three catches for 33 yards. "They didn't do anything special. We stopped ourselves. ... It shouldn't have been close. If we would have executed, it wouldn't have been a close game, but you've got to give credit when it's due. They found a way to win, but we'll go on to next week."

Late in the second quarter, Flacco hit Anquan Boldin for back-to-back lengthy completions down the sideline, the second one going for a 28-yard touchdown pass and a 13-3 Ravens lead. However, aside from that drive, the Ravens' fifth-year quarterback never looked comfortable against the league's top-ranked defense.

In a departure from his strong play at home this season, Flacco went 16-for-34 for 188 yards and the touchdown to Boldin. His biggest miscue came early in the fourth quarter after an end zone interception and daring return by Reed had given the Ravens the ball at their 27. On third-and-5, Flacco held on to the ball too long and was stripped by outside linebacker James Harrison.

Pittsburgh's Ziggy Hood recovered, and it took four plays — the final one being a 7-yard touchdown pass from Batch to tight end Heath Miller — for the Steelers to tie the game.

"Everybody was covered downfield. I was getting ready to tuck it and chalk it up as a loss. The guy came around and hit my wrist ... and just got it out. I tried to hold on, but I couldn't," Flacco said. "I think we hurt ourselves. That's the way I look at it."

With the game tied, the Ravens ran four plays on the following drive — none of which featured Rice, who finished with just 13 total touches — before having to punt the ball back to the Steelers.

Pittsburgh, which had eight turnovers the week before in an ugly loss to the Cleveland Browns, got the ball at its 15 with 6:14 to play. Batch (25-for-36 for 276 yards) hit Mike Wallace for gains of 15 and 7 yards.

Thriving with a short passing game, Batch found Antonio Brown for 4 and 9 yards. Then came the drive's biggest play: a 10-yard completion to Wallace coupled with a roughing-the-passer penalty on outside linebacker Paul Kruger that moved the ball to the Ravens 19.

"It was a big mistake on my part for even making it a possible call, and I just can't believe I put my teammates in that situation," Kruger said.

With only one timeout remaining, thanks in part to Harbaugh's acknowledged error in challenging an incompletion early in the third quarter, the Ravens watched as the Steelers got into position for Suisham to kick the game-winning field goal.

"I know what this team is all about," Boldin said. "A loss doesn't change who we are. We'll still go out, we'll win the AFC North, like I said, and we'll be a force to reckon with when the playoffs come." ■

Shaun Suisham kicks a 42-yard field goal as time expires to give the Steelers a 23-20 victory and end the Ravens' 16-game home winning streak.
Kenneth K. Lam | Baltimore Sun Photo

QUARTERBACK — D
Joe Flacco played at home the way he has on the road. He completed just 16 of 34 passes for 188 yards and threw one of his worst interceptions ever. Flacco twice underthrew Torrey Smith on long passes that could have been touchdowns, and he had a number of throws that were too high.

RUNNING BACKS — B
When it comes to offensive weapons, this group has the most consistent performers. Ray Rice makes an average offensive line look better, and rookie Bernard Pierce is a great complement when spelling Rice. Fullback Vonta Leach's blocks left a few Steelers feeling sore this morning.

RECEIVERS — C
Smith dropped several passes he should have caught, and Anquan Boldin spent more time complaining to officials than he did trying to get open, even though he had five catches for 81 yards, including a 31-yard TD. Anybody see tight end Dennis Pitta? He had one catch for 19 yards.

OFFENSIVE LINE — C-
The tackles had problems handling Pittsburgh's speed on the outside, and Flacco didn't help them by holding on to the ball too long. The Ravens couldn't handle the Steelers inside, and left guard Jah Reid has to stay on his feet. The Ravens might need to go back to Ramon Harewood.

DEFENSIVE LINE — C-
The Ravens were solid but didn't have any standouts. They could have done a better job of tackling. End Arthur Jones had four tackles, including one sack, and he had three QB hurries. The Ravens didn't get much from tackles Haloti Ngata or Ma'ake Kemoeatu, who combined for just two tackles.

LINEBACKERS — D
The Ravens were fine in run support even though inside linebacker Jameel McClain was sloppy tackling against the run. The Ravens might also need to work on getting deeper drops, especially in the middle of the field. McClain and outside linebacker Albert McClellan each had five tackles.

SECONDARY — D
When the Ravens played the Steelers two weeks ago, they were aggressive. The Ravens appeared to back off Sunday, and Pittsburgh hit a lot of short routes. The cornerbacks looked lost in zone coverage even though cornerback Cary Williams and safety Bernard Pollard turned in strong efforts.

SPECIAL TEAMS — B
As they have been most of the season, the coverage units were solid, but they couldn't pop any long returns the way they did against the Steelers two weeks ago. Jacoby Jones had problems fielding the ball but did return a kickoff 30 yards. Punter Sam Koch had a strong day.

COACHING — C
The Ravens' lack of discipline didn't cost them a week ago, but it did Sunday. Coach John Harbaugh needs to crack down on his team's whining. The Ravens spent a lot of time complaining to officials. Offensively, the Ravens had players open but failed to execute.

SCORING SUMMARY

1st Quarter
7:48 Pit FG Suisham 46

2nd Quarter
1:08 Bal FG Tucker 45
5:26 Bal FG Tucker 23
11:44 Bal TD Boldin 28 pass from Flacco (Tucker kick)
14:28 Pit FG Suisham 41

3rd Quarter
3:55 Pit TD Dwyer 16 run (Suisham kick)
10:10 Bal TD Rice 34 run (Tucker kick)

4th Quarter
7:36 Pit TD Miller 7 pass from Batch (Suisham kick)
15:00 Pit FG Suisham 42

DECEMBER 9, 2012	1	2	3	4	OT	F
RAVENS	7	14	0	7	0	28
REDSKINS	14	0	6	8	3	31

DONE IN BY ANOTHER BACKUP

BY JEFF ZREBIEC, THE BALTIMORE SUN

Rookie Cousins steps in for injured Griffin as 4th-quarter lead evaporates for 2nd game in row

LANDOVER — The player the Ravens had spent all week devising ways to contain was finally stopped. Robert Griffin III wasn't on the field after the Washington Redskins rookie took one more punishing hit in an afternoon filled with them, the last by Ravens defensive tackle Haloti Ngata injuring Griffin's knee and knocking him out of the game.

All the Ravens defense had to do was get one stop against a rookie backup quarterback, and a victory and a playoff berth would have been theirs. But that stop never came, and the Ravens were again forced to watch an opposing kicker split the uprights to seal their fate.

A week after Pittsburgh Steelers third-string quarterback Charlie Batch beat them, Redskins rookie backup Kirk Cousins tied the game with a touchdown pass and 2-point conversion with 29 seconds left in regulation. The Redskins then won it in overtime as Richard Crawford's 64-yard punt return set up Kai Forbath's game-winning 34-yard field goal in the Ravens' 31-28 loss in front of an announced 81,178 at FedEx Field.

Left tackle Michael Oher walks off the field in Landover after the Redskins dropped the Ravens' record to 9-4. Baltimore hadn't lost two straight games since 2009. *Kenneth K. Lam | Baltimore Sun Photo*

For the second straight week, the Ravens blew a fourth-quarter lead and were denied a chance to lock up a playoff berth; this time they missed an opportunity to clinch the AFC North. The Ravens are now 9-4 and losers of consecutive games for the first time since October 2009.

"It was tough to watch," said running back Ray Rice, who gave the Ravens a 28-20 lead with a 7-yard touchdown run with 4:47 left in the game. "I firmly believed that we had the game won, but we didn't."

With Griffin on the sideline after leading his team inside the Ravens 20, Cousins, a fourth-round pick out of Michigan State, hit Leonard Hankerson for

Kai Forbath celebrates with holder Sav Rocca after kicking a 34-yard field goal with 11:37 left in overtime to give the Redskins a 31-28 victory. The winning points were set up by Richard Crawford's 64-yard punt return.
Kenneth K. Lam | Baltimore Sun Photo

2013 SUPER BOWL CHAMPIONS

Redskins quarterback Robert Griffin III injures his right knee when tackled by defensive tackle Haloti Ngata after a 13-yard run late in the fourth quarter. *Kenneth K. Lam | Baltimore Sun Photo*

16 yards and then found Pierre Garcon alone in the end zone for an 11-yard touchdown. The Redskins needed a 2-point conversion to tie, but even with several Ravens defenders, including Ed Reed, calling out the quarterback draw, Cousins was able to take the snap and run it up the middle for the conversion.

The Ravens didn't get a first down on the first possession of overtime and then couldn't contain Crawford, who caught Sam Koch's 56-yard punt and sprinted around defenders until he ran out of gas and was tackled by Koch at the Ravens 24. Three plays later, Forbath ended a grueling back-and-forth game played in wet and sloppy conditions.

"They came in at a crucial time and made those plays at the end with the backup quarterback making those throws," Reed said. "We knew [Cousins' quarterback draw] was coming, which was crazy, but we have to execute at the end of the day. ...

It came down to one play executing. That's all that mattered."

While the loss may have been deflating for the Ravens, they did not lose any ground in the standings. The Steelers and the Cincinnati Bengals were both beaten Sunday, meaning that the Ravens still have a two-game lead with three to play in the AFC North. However, the Ravens' chances for a first-round bye continue to fade. Depending on what happens this evening between the New England Patriots and Houston Texans — the top two seeds in the AFC — the Ravens could be seeded as low as fourth in the conference heading into next week.

The Denver Broncos, who are 10-3 and will be at M&T Bank Stadium on Sunday, have passed the Ravens and now share the same record as the Indianapolis Colts.

"I don't know if people want me to be [ticked] off or" what, said Ravens wide receiver Anquan Boldin, who caught two touchdown passes in the first half. "We're still going to be a playoff

team. We're still going to win the [AFC] North. What else can I say? We let one get away today."

In the process, the Ravens might have also lost a couple of key performers. Right guard Marshal Yanda, the team's best offensive lineman, sprained his right ankle in overtime and left the stadium in a walking boot and on crutches. Inside linebacker Jameel McClain left the game in the third quarter with a neck injury.

The physical toll added to the frustration in the locker room as reality set in that the Ravens did virtually everything that they wanted to do against the Redskins (7-6) and they still lost.

"I think we should have won this game," said linebacker Paul Kruger, who had 1.5 of the Ravens' three sacks. "It's just a killer to come down here, play hard, play a full game and lose the way we did."

On offense, quarterback Joe Flacco broke from his struggles to complete 16 of 21 passes for

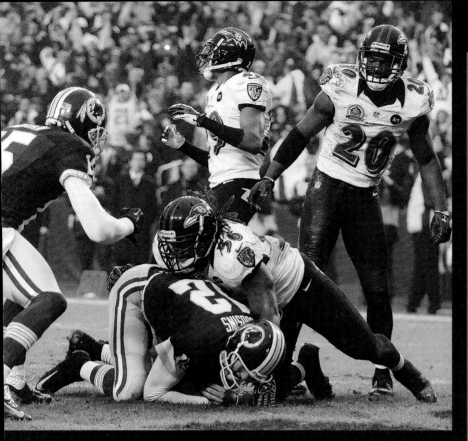

Redskins wide receiver Josh Morgan (15) reacts as backup quarterback Kirk Cousins (12) slips beneath linebacker Josh Bynes to tie the game with a 2-point conversion in the final minute of regulation. Cary Williams (29) and Ed Reed (20) react in disbelief. *Kenneth K. Lam | Baltimore Sun Photo*

MIKE PRESTON'S REPORT CARD

QUARTERBACK — C
Joe Flacco threw for 182 yards and had a quarterback rating of 121.4, but he had two costly turnovers. He still struggles with pocket awareness and doesn't know when to step up in the pocket. Flacco started the season off strong but has returned to his old inconsistent form.

RUNNING BACKS — B+
Ray Rice had 20 carries for 121 yards, and Bernard Pierce had 53 yards on eight carries, his most extensive action of the season. Both players ran hard and had good cutback runs. They were close to breaking a few long ones.

RECEIVERS — B-
Anquan Boldin had two touchdown receptions and tortured Washington cornerback DeAngelo Hall, especially with double moves. Tight end Dennis Pitta had a strong day, but the Ravens didn't get much from Torrey Smith, who had one catch for 21 yards.

OFFENSIVE LINE — C+
The Ravens ran for 186 yards against one of the better run defenses in the NFL, but their tackles struggled with Washington's outside pressure and got no help from Flacco about stepping up in the pocket. Like Flacco, this group had a strong first half but faded in the second.

DEFENSIVE LINE — B
This group looked lethargic at the beginning of the game but started to wear down the Redskins in the second half. The Ravens had to be disciplined, and they were. They kept good pressure on Robert Griffin III, who got hit often in the final two quarters.

LINEBACKERS — D
Outside linebacker Paul Kruger had a strong game and came down the line of scrimmage well. Inside linebacker Jameel McClain finished with eight tackles but missed a bunch. The Ravens also failed to wrap up, and this group can't cover downfield.

SECONDARY — C
This group played well in the second half but didn't deliver when it mattered most. The Ravens gave up big receptions over the middle, and they missed a lot of tackles on running plays. They don't have a thumper at safety, and only Cary Williams seems somewhat reliable at cornerback.

SPECIAL TEAMS — B
Return specialist Jacoby Jones gave the Ravens decent field position, and the Ravens' cover units played well. But the Ravens gave up a 64-yard punt return in overtime that led to the game-winning field goal. That's a big no-no.

COACHING — B
Overall, it was a solid game plan. The defense did a decent job and got stronger in the second half. Offensively, the Ravens stayed with their game plan and attacked the Redskins with the run. They were ready to play and well-prepared. This loss is on the players.

three touchdowns, 182 yards and a 121.5 quarterback rating. Against the NFL's fourth-ranked rushing defense, the Ravens ran for 186 yards. Rice had 121 of them, eclipsing the 100-yard mark for the first time since Week 5.

On defense, the Ravens were gouged for 186 first-quarter yards — a league high this year for any team — and two touchdowns. But after that, the Ravens, playing without Terrell Suggs, mostly controlled Griffin and hit him at every opportunity.

Still, the Ravens made too many mistakes. Flacco committed two turnovers — a fumble and an interception — in the third quarter, and both led to field goals by Forbath. On the interception, the Ravens had the ball at the Redskins 11 and figured they would at least end up with a field-goal attempt. But Flacco was hit by linebacker

Ryan Kerrigan, and his pass fluttered up the middle and into the arms of Washington's London Fletcher.

For as well as the Ravens played defensively, they allowed the Redskins to drive 85 yards on 13 plays to get the tying touchdown and conversion. Redskins receivers ran free in the secondary throughout the drive, with the final miscue coming when Chris Johnson lost Pierre Garcon in the back of the end zone.

Cousins went 2-for-2 for 26 yards on the final drive and also got a pass-interference call on Johnson.

"Obviously, it's a frustrating situation, especially to allow a backup rookie to come in and make plays the way he did," cornerback Cary Williams said. "It's frustrating, but we got to find a way to win. Good teams find a way, and we didn't."■

SCORING SUMMARY

1st Quarter
5:22 Was TD Morgan 4 pass from Griffin III (Forbath kick)
7:55 Bal TD Boldin 19 pass from Flacco (Tucker kick)
12:05 Was TD Morris 1 run (Forbath kick)

2nd Quarter
4:44 Bal TD Boldin 31 pass from Flacco (Tucker kick)
6:21 Bal TD Pitta 14 pass from Flacco (Tucker kick)

3rd Quarter
4:33 Was FG Forbath 48
13:39 Was FG Forbath 49

4th Quarter
10:13 Bal TD Rice 7 run (Tucker kick)
14:31 Was TD Garcon 11 pass from Cousins (Cousins run)

Overtime
3:23 Was FG Forbath 34

DECEMBER 16, 2012	1	2	3	4	F
BRONCOS	3	14	14	3	34
RAVENS	0	0	3	14	17

SLOUCHING INTO THE PLAYOFFS

BY JEFF ZREBIEC, THE BALTIMORE SUN

Slump continues, but Pittsburgh loss guarantees Ravens their fifth straight postseason berth

The signs of frustration and desperation were everywhere at M&T Bank Stadium, which had so many empty seats by the middle of the fourth quarter Sunday that it felt like a preseason game.

Ed Reed slammed down and then kicked his helmet on the sideline after Denver Broncos wide receiver Eric Decker grabbed a 51-yard touchdown. Torrey Smith yelled in the direction of a trainer when he was told he was done for the day with concussion-like symptoms. Cary Williams and Anquan Boldin drew penalty flags for illegal hits. Michael Oher walked off the field, grumbling about why the Ravens were throwing the ball in the game's final seconds, resulting in two Broncos sacks.

But if there was one image that encapsulated the Ravens' 34-17 loss to the Broncos — their third straight defeat and the second straight at home — it was quarterback Joe Flacco's 80-yard sprint and unsuccessful lunge at the legs of cornerback Chris Harris.

For the Ravens, securing a division title again proved just as elusive as Harris in what might have

Wide receiver Jacoby Jones (12) and running back Ray Rice appear deflated on the sideline after cornerback Chris Harris' 98-yard interception return gave the Broncos a 16-0 lead with 15 seconds left in the first half.
Karl Merton Ferron | Baltimore Sun Photo

Quarterback Joe Flacco is kicked in the chest as he tries in vain to stop Chris Harris' interception return. Flacco's pass to the left corner of the end zone never reached wide receiver Anquan Boldin. *Karl Merton Ferron | Baltimore Sun Photo*

been the game's turning point. Harris' 98-yard interception return for a touchdown just before halftime spearheaded a Broncos rout and capped another disappointing performance for Flacco and the offense.

The only positive came hours later when the Dallas Cowboys beat the Pittsburgh Steelers, 27-24, in overtime, clinching the Ravens' fifth straight playoff berth. The Ravens have a one-game lead in the AFC North over the Cincinnati Bengals and a two-game advantage over the Steelers, putting them in good position to defend their AFC North title. The Bengals play the Steelers next week, and a Pittsburgh victory, coupled with a Ravens win over the New York Giants next Sunday at M&T Bank Stadium, would give the Ravens the division title.

But the Ravens didn't look much like a playoff team Sunday.

"We're a 9-5 football team, and it feels like we're 0-14 right now," said Flacco, who completed 20 of 40 passes for two touchdowns, turned the ball over twice and gained most of his 254 passing yards when the game was out of reach. "That's just the feeling that you have right after a game like this. It's going to test a lot of things in us guys. We believe we're pretty stand-up guys, tough guys, guys with character. We're going to be able to look at ourselves in the mirror when this thing is all said and done and honestly say that we are those types of guys or that we're not."

As he spoke, blood collected on the right side of Flacco's face, courtesy of several Broncos hits on him during the afternoon. He's hardly the only Raven who looks beaten up and lost, struggling with confidence and unable to figure out why a once-comfortable lead in the AFC North is now down to one game over the Cincinnati Bengals.

The Ravens have lost three straight games for the first time since October 2009. They have dropped back-to-back home games for the first time in the John Harbaugh era, and Sunday's loss was their most lopsided defeat at M&T Bank Stadium since Peyton Manning's Indianapolis Colts beat them, 44-20, on Dec. 9, 2007.

This time it was Manning's Broncos doing the damage, overwhelming the injury-depleted and mistake-prone Ravens in every facet of the game. Denver, which has won nine straight to improve to 11-3, led 17-0 at halftime and 31-3 at the end of the third quarter. By then, most of the announced 71,317 had hit the exits, leaving the first couple of rows of the stadium filled with orange.

"As a single player, as an individual, right now I am embarrassed to come out and perform the way we have," said Reed, who called punter Sam Koch, long snapper Morgan Cox and kicker Justin Tucker the Ravens' best three players in the game. "We're not the only team that lost today, and we still have two more games. But as a player, I am embarrassed for our city."

Manning's teams have now beaten the Ravens nine straight times, but this latest one went far beyond the Broncos quarter-

Quarterback Joe Flacco fumbles as he's hit by former Ravens defensive tackle Justin Bannan, right, early in the first quarter. Broncos safety Rahim Moore recovered at the Denver 47. *Lloyd Fox | Baltimore Sun Photo*

back, who was 17-for-28 for 204 yards and a touchdown and directed an offense that was plenty content to run the football.

There was Knowshon Moreno rushing for 118 yards and a score. There was Decker catching eight passes for 133 yards and a touchdown. There was the Broncos defense holding the Ravens without a first down for more than 24 minutes to start the game and limiting Pro Bowl running back Ray Rice to 41 yards of offense. And there was Harris, stepping in front of Anquan Boldin right in front of

the goal line and running his interception to the end zone for the backbreaking touchdown.

"I didn't really expect him to throw that out route, but he threw it to me and I just wanted to make sure I scored," Harris said. "That was a long run, but once I got to the 40, I was like, 'I just have to stride it on in.' "

Flacco was booed as he jogged back onto the field to take a knee and again as he headed into the locker room at halftime. At the very least, the Ravens should have gone into the locker room trailing no worse than 10-3 after a half in which they were dominated.

"It's kind of like calling a timeout in that situation because it's one of those things that you catch it and get out of bounds, you catch it in the end zone, or you throw it away and you live for the next down," Flacco said. "I just made a mistake."

Harbaugh said he considered calling a timeout after Smith's 14-yard catch got the ball to the 4-yard line. However, Harbaugh liked the play call and didn't want to give Manning too much time if the Broncos were to get the ball back.

"That's [the] coach's call. That's my call," Harbaugh said. "We run that a lot. We've done that a lot this year. We've done it over the last few years. There's a number of play calls that we have in that situation. Joe is trying to stick it in there for a touchdown. The kid [Harris] made a great play. That's what happens. That's football."

The Ravens finally got on the board on their first drive of the second half when Tucker kicked a 45-yard field goal. But Manning needed just five plays to get the Broncos back into the end zone, hitting Decker in stride down the left sideline for the 51-yard score. On the play, Reed was caught in no man's land and Williams was just beaten.

"This team is in a slump," Williams said. "When you're in a slump, you try not to point fingers."

The Broncos got the ball back after another Ravens three-and-out and needed just four plays this time to score as Moreno was virtually untouched on a 6-yard touchdown run that made it 31-3 and started the stadium exodus.

"This is our loss, no less than the last three losses were our losses," Harbaugh said. "We didn't get a very fast start. We had some self-inflicted issues around halftime. We couldn't get anything until late, so that's where we're at. We understand that. We are going to work to improve. The most important thing to understand is that every goal that we have — starting with our first goal, which is to win the AFC North — is in front of us. It's still there, and every dream that we have, [including] the ultimate dream, is still available to us."

But with two games left — Sunday against the Giants and then the following week against the Bengals — much will have to change for the Ravens to look like legitimate contenders. The defense played without its top three linebackers in Ray Lewis, Jameel McClain and Dannell Ellerbe, while outside linebacker Terrell Suggs' effectiveness was limited by a torn right biceps.

The offense was without Pro Bowl right guard Marshal Yanda and tight end Ed Dickson, and then it lost Smith (Maryland) and backup running back Bernard Pierce to concussions, and wide receiver Tandon Doss to an ankle injury.

"It feels awful, but it's about the team that gets hot right now," Rice said. "We're banged up. We are trying to find our way back healthy right now. All we need to do is get one win. There is no sugarcoating. ... It's late in the year. It's not getting any easier. We either put it on our shoulders, get it fixed or we'll weed ourselves out like the other teams in the league." ∎

MIKE PRESTON'S REPORT CARD

QUARTERBACK — F
Joe Flacco has poor mechanics. He isn't stepping into his throws and is instead throwing off his back foot. He is dropping his elbow again when he throws. He had two major turnovers, and the 98-yard interception at the end of half turned the momentum of the game.

RUNNING BACKS — D
Ray Rice seems to be hesitating when he hits the hole, and he spent more time drifting than accelerating. Backup Bernard Pierce was more aggressive, but his time was cut short because of a concussion. Pierce's style seems better suited for the Ravens because he makes one cut and runs.

RECEIVERS — F
The Ravens did get outstanding catches, from Torrey Smith and Jacoby Jones, but they weren't consistent as a group. By the third quarter, some of them were jogging short routes across the middle, especially with Flacco misfiring. Tight end Dennis Pitta was the only bright spot.

OFFENSIVE LINE — D
Tackles Michael Oher and Kelechi Osemele couldn't handle the speed, and left guard Jah Reid still has problems staying on his feet. Without right guard Marshal Yanda, the Ravens now have one of the weakest offensive lines in the NFL.

DEFENSIVE LINE — F
This group made Denver running back Knowshon Moreno look like Terrell Davis. The entire unit got pushed around, especially tackles Terrence Cody and end DeAngelo Tyson. They couldn't get off blocks or work off double teams. They stood up too high.

LINEBACKERS — F
The inside linebackers looked like giant redwoods being chopped down. There was too much fighting with blockers instead of shedding them, and there were times when the Ravens were physically dominated.

SECONDARY — F
Some of the poor play was the result of a lack of pressure, but cornerback Cary Williams will be seeing a lot of double moves in his sleep. For the third straight week, the Ravens gave up big yards in the middle of the field. Safety Ed Reed appears to be playing in his own world these days.

SPECIAL TEAMS — B
Punter Sam Koch, kicker Justin Tucker, returner Jacoby Jones and long snapper Morgan Cox were the Ravens' best players

COACHING — D-
No offense, no defense and no excitement. Where was the up-tempo offense? Where was the innovative defense? Only the special teams showed up.

SCORING SUMMARY

1st Quarter
7:47 Den FG Prater 27

2nd Quarter
3:09 Den TD Hester 1 run (Prater kick)
14:45 Den TD Harris 98 int. return (Prater kick)

3rd Quarter
2:42 Bal FG Tucker 45
5:07 Den TD Decker 51 pass from P. Manning (Prater kick)
7:20 Den TD Moreno 6 run (Prater kick)

4th Quarter
0:29 Bal TD Pitta 31 pass from Flacco (Tucker kick)
10:28 Den FG Prater 36
10:52 Bal TD Pitta 61 pass from Flacco (Tucker kick)

DECEMBER 23, 2012	1	2	3	4	F
GIANTS	7	0	0	7	14
RAVENS	14	10	3	6	33

'WE'RE HERE TO STAY'

BY JEFF ZREBIEC, THE BALTIMORE SUN

Ravens end 3–game slide, clinch AFC North, begin to build momentum for postseason

Center Matt Birk and team owner Steve Bisciotti celebrate after the Ravens embarrassed the defending Super Bowl champion Giants and earned the right to host a playoff game. *Lloyd Fox | Baltimore Sun Photo*

The shaky, mistake-prone quarterback morphed into a precise passer. An offense that hadn't consistently moved the ball for weeks chewed up yardage at will. A defense that had given up ground for much of the season had a two-time Super Bowl-winning quarterback on the run.

Nothing the Ravens had done in the past month foreshadowed their 33-14 throttling of the New York Giants on Sunday in front of an announced 71,470, the second-biggest crowd in M&T Bank Stadium history.

Picking a fine time to play their best all-around game of the season, the Ravens overwhelmed the reigning Super Bowl champions in every way. When it was over, the Ravens celebrated the end of their three-game losing streak, their second consecutive AFC North crown and the right to host a first-round playoff game.

"Like I said last week, we're going to see what kind of team we are," said quarterback Joe Flacco, who broke from a disturbing trend of uneven play to complete 25 of 36 passes for 309 yards and two touchdowns without a turnover. "We believe we're this kind of team, and we're really going to see if we are. I think that we showed ourselves and we showed people today that we are that kind of team. We're here to stay, and we just have to do all we can to get better than this throughout the re-maining weeks."

If the New England Patriots lose to the Miami Dolphins next week and the Ravens (10-5) beat the Cincinnati Bengals in the regular-season finale, the Ravens could still earn the No. 3 seed and a home date in two weeks against the Bengals, who

Running back Bernard Pierce eludes Giants linebackers Spencer Paysinger (52) and Chase Blackburn for a first down. Pierce gained 123 yards on 14 carries. *Gene Sweeney Jr.* | *Baltimore Sun Photo*

Linebacker Dannell Ellerbe celebrates a sack of the Giants' Eli Manning in the first quarter. Manning was held to 150 passing yards. *Gene Sweeney Jr.* | *Baltimore Sun Photo*

are locked into the sixth spot. However, with a Patriots win or Ravens loss, the Ravens would host the fifth-seeded Indianapolis Colts in two weeks.

Those scenarios — and how the Ravens will handle next Sunday's game in Cincinnati if nothing is on the line — will be discussed plenty during the next few days. For now, though, the Ravens were consumed not only by their accomplishment — they had never won back-to-back division titles in team history — but also by the manner in which they obtained it.

"I'm not rating challenges, but I am as proud of this team right now as ever," said Ravens coach John Harbaugh, whose team avoided what would have been its first four-game losing streak in his tenure. "We've said this before [but] I love this team, I

love every single guy on this team. I love the way they compete, I love the way they work, the way they fight. This is just a really special group of men. How far we take each other, we'll find out [but] for them to earn a championship like this means a lot."

In building a lead of 24-7 at halftime and 33-7 in the fourth quarter, the Ravens set season highs in net yards (533) and rushing yards (224) with Ray Rice and Bernard Pierce gaining more than 100 each on the ground.

Dominating both lines of scrimmage, they won the time-of-possession battle, 39:21 to 20:39. They held two-time Super Bowl Most Valuable Player Eli Manning to 150 passing yards, with one late meaningless touchdown pass, and sacked him three times. They limited the prolific wide receiver tandem of Victor Cruz and Ha-

keem Nicks to three catches for 21 yards (all by Cruz), and they allowed the Giants just 67 yards on the ground.

The Giants (8-7), who now need a lot of help next week to make the playoffs, were supposed to be the more desperate team because the Ravens had already clinched a playoff berth. However, it was the Ravens who played with urgency.

If the Ravens entered the game looking like one of the more vulnerable teams in the AFC playoff picture, they exited it looking capable of putting a run together in January.

"I just think we had a little bit more sense of urgency because we knew what was at stake," said Rice, who rushed for 107 yards and caught six passes for 51 yards, including a 27-yard touchdown. "This was a championship

Wide receiver Torrey Smith hangs on the crossbar after his 6-yard touchdown reception in the first quarter put the Ravens ahead 7-0.
Gene Sweeney Jr. | *Baltimore Sun Photo*

game for us. Next week, we understand what that game is, but this was the championship for us. This was [to] solidify the home playoff game, back-to-back division champs. That's huge around here. We'll humble ourselves, we'll enjoy this week, and we'll get back to work ... but playoff football essentially started today."

After lacking a rhythm for several weeks, the Ravens offense played with confidence, speed and explosiveness. Wide receiver Torrey Smith (Maryland), who was questionable for the game after suffering a concussion last week, had a 6-yard touchdown catch on the Ravens' first possession and set up Flacco's 1-yard touchdown run on the next drive with a 43-yard catch.

Two drives later, a 39-yard completion from Flacco to Anquan Boldin on third-and-18 set up the first of four field goals by Justin Tucker. On their next drive, Flacco hit Smith for 21 yards and Boldin for 12 before hitting Rice on a slant pattern for the 27-yard score.

"When Joe is in a zone, he's one of the best quarterbacks," tight end Ed Dickson said. "I thought Joe stepped up big and

showed a little emotion today. I thought he was in the zone."

Flacco hit seven receivers and compiled a 114.2 quarterback rating. It was the first time in four games that he passed for more than 300 yards and did not commit a turnover. Flacco had turned the ball over six times over his previous three games but provided plenty of time, he didn't put the ball in harm's way at all against a defense that had made 20 interceptions.

Aside from seeing a two-touchdown lead cut to 14-7 on David Wilson's 14-yard touchdown run late in the first quarter, the Ravens were barely threatened by the Giants, who have now been outscored 67-14 over their past two games.

"Oh, man, this one was good," said linebacker Dannell Ellerbe, who returned after missing three games with an ankle injury. "The way the offense was making plays today, and the fact that we are getting guys healthy now, that's going to be the big key for our future heading into the playoffs. If we can keep our guys healthy, we will be good in January."■

SCORING SUMMARY

1st Quarter
7:22   Bal   TD   T. Smith 6 pass from Flacco (Tucker kick)
10:36   Bal   TD   Flacco 1 run (Tucker kick)
13:30   NYG   TD   Wilson 14 run (Tynes kick)

2nd Quarter
8:55   Bal   FG   Tucker 23
13:56   Bal   TD   Rice 27 pass from Flacco (Tucker kick)

3rd Quarter
9:42   Bal   FG   Tucker 21

4th Quarter
3:52   Bal   FG   Tucker 30
7:35   Bal   FG   Tucker 29
11:42   NYG   TD   Hixon 13 pass from Manning (Tynes kick)

DECEMBER 30, 2012	1	2	3	4	F
RAVENS	7	0	0	10	17
BENGALS	0	7	6	10	23

PLAYING IT SAFE IN FINALE

BY JEFF ZREBIEC, THE BALTIMORE SUN

With playoff spot clinched, Ravens pull starters early to concentrate on getting healthy

Cornerback Chykie Brown puts his hands to his helmet after a 44-yard reception by wide receiver Brandon Tate gives the Bengals the ball at the Ravens 21, setting up the go-ahead field goal in the fourth quarter. *Gene Sweeney Jr.* | *Baltimore Sun Photo*

CINCINNATI —The Ravens starters who did suit up for Sunday's regular-season finale began heading to the sideline about midway through the first quarter. Pro Bowl running back Ray Rice went first, pulling on a winter cap and a black jacket. Quarterback Joe Flacco followed him a couple of minutes later after playing two uneventful series.

By the early stages of the second quarter, they were joined by wide receiver Torrey Smith (Maryland), center Matt Birk, cornerback Cary Williams and safety Ed Reed.

With an AFC North title and a home playoff game next weekend already secured, the Ravens treated their regular-season finale at Paul Brown Stadium like a preseason game. The result — a 23-17 loss to the Cincinnati Bengals in front of an announced 61,565 on a frigid afternoon — hardly mattered.

All that appeared to matter to the Ravens was staying healthy — a feat that they seemed to accomplish — and setting themselves up to be at their best when the In-dianapolis Colts come to M&T Bank Stadium next weekend for a wild-card playoff game.

The fourth-seeded Ravens and fifth-seeded Colts will play at 1 p.m. Sunday at M&T Bank Stadium.

"The goal was twofold: to put ourselves in the best position possible going forward into the playoffs and to win the game," said Ravens coach John Harbaugh, who substituted his starters much more quickly than did Bengals coach Marvin Lewis. "We obviously didn't win the game and we're disappointed with that, but we feel like we're in the best position we could have been going forward in the playoffs. That's really all that matters."

Linebacker Dannell Ellerbe (59), defensive tackle Bryan Hall (95) and linebacker Paul Kruger celebrate a sack of Bengals backup Bruce Gradkowski. Both teams used reserve players for much of the game to rest their regulars for the playoffs. *Gene Sweeney Jr.* | *Baltimore Sun Photo*

2013 SUPER BOWL CHAMPIONS

Like the Bengals, the Ravens finished the regular season with a 10-6 record. But the Ravens won their second straight AFC North championship because they had a better divisional mark (4-2) than Cincinnati (3-3). Because the Ravens won their division, they will host in the first round even though the Colts have the better record at 11-5.

Riding the strong play of rookie quarterback Andrew Luck and the emotion of head coach and former Ravens defensive co-ordinator Chuck Pagano's return after treatment for leukemia, the Colts have won five of their past six games and nine of their past 11. That includes a 28-16 victory over Houston on Sunday in a game that the Texans needed to win to secure a first-round bye and home-field advantage throughout the playoffs.

Meanwhile, the Ravens have dropped four of their past five games and barely played any of their regulars in Sunday's loss to the Bengals, which was sealed when defensive end Carlos Dunlap intercepted backup quarterback Tyrod Taylor's pass and returned it 14 yards for a touchdown with 6:06 to play.

"Yeah, it's a loss, [but] this game is totally different than any of the other games," Ravens cornerback Corey Graham said. "You don't really look at it that way. This is more of a get healthy, get ready for the playoffs. Some losses mean more than others, and this one here don't mean a lot."

Graham maintained that the Ravens are in great position to start a playoff run, an opinion echoed throughout the locker room.

"AFC North champions, I'll just say that," Rice said. "We battled adversity, we battled injury and we battled everything else you can imagine for a football team. I'm not really concerned about the losses. I'm more con-

Backup Tyrod Taylor is sacked by Bengals defensive end Wallace Gilberry for a 10-yard loss late in the fourth quarter. Taylor completed 15 of 25 passes for 149 yards. *Kenneth K. Lam | Baltimore Sun Photo*

cerned about this team getting healthy. We are going to hit our stride going into the playoffs."

The Ravens talked all week about Sunday's game still having significance even though they were content with where they stood. They also knew even if they had beaten the Bengals, it would still take a Miami Dolphins victory over the New England Patriots at Gillette Stadium for them to finish as the No. 3 seed. The Patriots wound up winning that game, 28-0.

So Harbaugh rested veterans Anquan Boldin, Marshal Yanda, Ray Lewis, Terrell Suggs, Haloti Ngata and Bernard Pollard. All are expected to face the Colts. So are fullback Vonta Leach and right tackle Kelechi Osemele, who were both removed from Sunday's game

early after getting nicked up.

Rice played just one series, rushing three times for 5 yards and committing a personal foul that took the Ravens out of field-goal range. Flacco played just two series, completing four of eight passes for 34 yards and getting sacked once.

"It's an accomplishment to be in a position where you can afford to do that," Harbaugh said. "If we would have been playing for more, then we would have played them. If we had an opportunity to move up dramatically in the seeding, then we would have done that. I thought our guys did a good job, we got some young guys some experience. There are always positives to be found in that. You just

Running back Bernard Pierce is dropped for a 3-yard loss by Bengals defensive ends Wallace Gilberry, left, and Carlos Dunlap. Dunlap's late interception return for a touchdown put the game away for Cincinnati.
Gene Sweeney Jr. | Baltimore Sun Photo

MIKE PRESTON'S REPORT CARD

QUARTERBACK — C
Joe Flacco threw only eight passes but had little chance to get into a rhythm. Backup Tyrod Taylor was just as inaccurate but made plays with his legs, which is expected from a backup. The interception late in the game was a backbreaker, and he almost had another.

RUNNING BACKS — B
Rookie Bernard Pierce played well and made good decisions quickly as he finished with 89 yards on 22 carries. He basically was the Ravens' offense for the first three quarters. Backup Anthony Allen played well, and the Ravens got a lot of production without fullback Vonta Leach.

RECEIVERS — C-
This group didn't contribute much until late in the game. The Ravens didn't activate starter Anquan Boldin and got Torrey Smith off the field early. Jacoby Jones and tight end Ed Dickson made contributions, but this group provided little impact.

OFFENSIVE LINE — C
Never has a right guard meant so much to a team: The Ravens are weak when Marshal Yanda doesn't play. Michael Oher was decent moving from left tackle to right, and rookie center Gino Gradkowski held his own. But the Ravens allowed too much pressure on Taylor.

DEFENSIVE LINE — B
The Ravens held the Bengals to 49 rushing yards, and they got big plays from Ma'ake Kemoeatu (four tackles), Bryan Hall and Arthur Jones (five tackles). The Ravens put pressure on the Bengals quarterbacks and forced them to move from the pocket.

LINEBACKERS — B
Dannell Ellerbe had six tackles, including two for losses. He is going to cost the Ravens big money to re-sign this offseason. Inside linebacker Josh Bynes had nine, and the Ravens kept the Bengals from getting outside. For a patched-up crew, they also covered passes decently.

SECONDARY — B
The Ravens did a good job of shutting down Bengals receiver A.J. Green early. Ravens cornerbacks did a nice job of locking onto the receivers but gave up yardage over the middle in zone coverage. Cornerback Jimmy Smith showed improvement from previous games.

SPECIAL TEAMS — C
The Bengals did a good job of controlling Jacoby Jones on punt returns. Sam Koch might have had his worst day in his seven years in the league, averaging 36.6 yards on seven punts. Justin Tucker was 1-for-2 on field-goal tries.

COACHING — D
The big question of the week is whether coach John Harbaugh would have pulled his starters so quickly if the Ravens had been at home. All week he kept saying he was playing to win, but his starters didn't get much playing time. Next time, just fess up.

can't predict how it's all going to play out necessarily. The guys that we sat down, for the most part, were ... injury situations. It started with Marshal and the offensive line, so once you start pulling Marshal back because that's best for him going forward, then you have to consider Joe and Ray and stuff like that."

Getting the first extensive regular-season action of his career, Taylor relieved Flacco late in the first quarter and directed a scoring drive completed by Anthony Allen's 2-yard touchdown run. It was the first score of Allen's career.

Taylor's first career touchdown, a 1-yard scramble early in the fourth quarter, gave the Ravens a 14-13 lead. However, Josh Brown put the Bengals ahead with a 38-yard field goal and then Dunlap ended any

doubt with the interception return for a touchdown. Taylor completed 15 of 25 passes for 149 yards and an interception and rushed nine times for 65 yards and a touchdown.

About 45 minutes after the game, several Ravens still weren't sure whom they'd play this weekend until they were notified by reporters. The news was bittersweet to Reed, who is extremely close with Colts wide receiver Reggie Wayne and Pagano, who recruited the safety to the University of Miami.

"Chuck is like a dad to me. It means a lot," said Reed, who acknowledged that he exchanged text messages with Pagano on Christmas. "I'd much rather see them in the AFC championship game than the first week, but they're men just like us." ▪

SCORING SUMMARY

1st Quarter
14:43 Bal   TD   Allen 2 run (Tucker kick)

2nd Quarter
14:21 Cin   TD   Jones 11 pass from Dalton (Brown kick)

3rd Quarter
8:45   Cin   FG   Brown 47
12:36 Cin   FG   Brown 32

4th Quarter
2:10   Bal   TD   Taylor 1 run (Tucker kick)
7:44   Cin   FG   Brown 38
8:54   Cin   TD   Dunlap 14 int. return (Brown kick)
13:39 Bal   FG   Tucker 49

RAY LEWIS

BY MIKE PRESTON, THE BALTIMORE SUN

No. 52 departs as the greatest ever to play middle linebacker

There is really only one more appropriate ending for Ray Lewis, and that won't come for five more years, when he takes his place in the Pro Football Hall of Fame as the greatest middle linebacker ever.

Lewis, 37, announced Wednesday [Jan. 2] that he will retire at the end of the Ravens' season, and even though it was a sad day for Baltimore sports fans, it was a great one, too.

Unlike Johnny Unitas, the city's other legendary football player, Lewis gets to end his career in a Baltimore uniform. No other hometown fan base will be revved up by his introductory dance, which will be on display one more time Sunday when the Ravens host the Indianapolis Colts in an AFC wild-card game at M&T Bank Stadium.

Often in sports we use the word "great," but that should be reserved for players who transcend the game and reinvent their position.

That was Ray Lewis, No. 52.

There have been other great ones, such as the Chicago Bears' Dick Butkus and Mike Singletary, but none was the complete package like Lewis.

"I think Butkus was the best at stopping the run, but Ray Lewis could stop the run or get back in to play pass defense," said former Baltimore Colts running back Tom Matte, who played against most of the top middle linebackers. "He had such speed and agility. I'm prejudiced, of course, but there was none better.

"I'm happy to see him retiring as a Raven. He is the last of a dying breed, a player who never wanted to play anywhere else."

Lewis was exceptional because he was the first middle linebacker who could run sideline to sideline and still cover a tight end or running back one-on-one down the field. He studied and prepared for every game as if it were his last, and he made others around him great.

It didn't seem as though Lewis would make this

Linebacker Ray Lewis expresses his feeling to fans after coming out of his last game at M&T Bank Stadium during the postseason. *Kenneth K. Lam | Baltimore Sun Photo*

incredible Hall of Fame journey when he arrived in Baltimore 17 years ago. On his first day here, he sat in the hall at the team's old training facility in Owings Mills wearing dark sunglasses, a blue pinstriped suit and gold chains around his neck. He looked like he weighed about 220 pounds.

"That is going to be your middle linebacker?" I asked Ravens general manager Ozzie Newsome. "Damn, he is skinny."

"Yes," Newsome replied. "Wait till you see the finished product."

Since then, he has been selected to 13 Pro Bowls, won a Super Bowl, been named Super Bowl Most Valuable Player and received two NFL Defensive Player of the Year Awards. Lewis is just the sixth player in NFL history to win Player of the Year more than once, and the only middle linebacker other than Singletary.

And here's something else that separates Lewis from the others: He played 17 years. Few of the great ones come close to his longevity.

There are other intangibles that made Lewis great. When Lewis was in his prime, Ravens coaches Ted Marchibroda and Brian Billick had to slow him in practice because he always played at game speed.

Lewis challenged his teammates to be great and often delivered "boomalachers," the famed speech titled "Where

Would You Rather Be?" before big games.

"He never disappointed," said Cincinnati Bengals head coach Marvin Lewis, Lewis' first defensive coordinator in Baltimore. "He always said he wanted to learn the game as a coach, and he was motivated to be the best. He made everybody else better, and he took the leadership role on his shoulders even as a young player."

Through 17 years, Lewis left a trail of battered bodies. In 2008, Lewis tackled Pittsburgh Steelers running back Rashard Mendenhall so hard that he broke Mendenhall's collarbone. Against Cincinnati in 2000, Lewis was so destructive on the field that running back Corey Dillon declined to go back into the game late in the fourth quarter.

The turning point in Ray Lewis' career came Sept. 29, 1997, when San Diego Chargers running back Eric Metcalf caught a pass in the

left flat and darted over the middle. Lewis changed direction and ran down Metcalf after a 62-yard gain.

Metcalf had been timed in the 40-yard dash in 4.3 seconds, but Lewis caught him and pulled him down with one hand. Middle linebackers weren't supposed to run that fast.

That's when you knew the Ravens had something special in No. 52.

Through the years, I've had a good relationship with Lewis. There have been some rocky times in the past couple of seasons because I saw a player starting to lose some attributes that had made him great.

But in every practice I've attended since the team moved here for the 1996 season, and there have been many, I always took some time to watch Lewis and, until he retired, future Hall of Fame offensive tackle Jonathan Ogden.

That was my privilege, my honor, to watch greatness at work.

I often wondered how this on-field marriage between Lewis and the Ravens would end. I didn't want to see him go out like Unitas, gimpy-legged and wearing a Chargers uniform.

I'm glad to see Lewis come back from injury. I'm glad he'll come out of the tunnel one more time to dance, because it's something we all can savor.

It's fitting for the fans, the city and Ray Lewis, the greatest middle linebacker ever to play the game.∎

Ray Lewis, who had unheard-of speed for a middle linebacker, crushes Browns wide receiver Dennis Northcutt after a catch in 2003. *Elizabeth Malby | Baltimore Sun Photo*

JANUARY 6, 2013	1	2	3	4	F
COLTS	0	6	3	0	9
RAVENS	0	10	7	7	24

FAREWELL IS ONLY THE BEGINNING

BY JEFF ZREBIEC, THE BALTIMORE SUN

Star linebacker Lewis' 13 tackles in final home game help send Ravens to second round of playoffs

Ray Lewis ran onto the field one more time, and the man who has written the Ravens' defensive record book had another career first left in him. As quarterback Joe Flacco prepared to kneel, Lewis jogged about 10 yards behind him and took his place in the victory formation.

Once Flacco took the final snap and handed the ball to referee Mike Carey, Lewis did his trademark dance. This was indeed Lewis' day. He had earned that much in the final home game of his 17 seasons, all with one franchise.

When it was over, the Ravens rushed onto the field to celebrate the continuation of not just Lewis' Hall of Fame-worthy career, but also their season. A 24-9 victory over the Indianapolis Colts in front of an announced 71,379 at M&T Bank Stadium sends the Ravens into the divisional round of the playoffs, where they will meet a Denver Broncos team that embarrassed them by 17 points in Baltimore three weeks ago.

The Ravens and Broncos will play at Sports Authority Field at

Members of Ravens Roost 35 of Annapolis ham it up in their Ray Lewis No. 52 jerseys during a pregame tailgate party outside M&T Bank Stadium.
Amy Davis | Baltimore Sun Photo

Mile High at 4:30 p.m. Saturday, and a win would get the Ravens into the AFC championship game for a second straight season. As it is, the Ravens have now won a playoff game for five straight seasons. John Harbaugh is the first coach since the 1970 AFL-NFL merger to earn a postseason victory in his first five seasons.

"I think we're all appreciative, grateful for the opportunity to be here and to witness this historic moment in sports," said Harbaugh,

who is 6-4 in the postseason, including 4-0 in wild-card games. "It wasn't just about one guy. Nobody understands it more than the one guy we're talking about. It was about a team. It was about a city, a fan base, about a great sport, about a great career. I'm just humbled to be part of it."

Lewis, who announced Wednesday that this playoff run would be his "last ride," took a victory lap around M&T Bank

Cornerback Cary Williams intercepts a pass at the Ravens 15 that was intended for Colts wide receiver Reggie Wayne (87) late in the fourth quarter. Williams returned the ball 41 yards. *Kenneth K. Lam | Baltimore Sun Photo*

Stadium reminiscent of former Oriole Cal Ripken Jr.'s celebration at Camden Yards after he broke Lou Gehrig's streak for consecutive major league baseball games played. In Lewis' first game since he tore his right triceps Oct. 14, he was credited with a game-high 13 tackles.

"It probably won't sink in," Lewis said when asked about never getting to play at M&T Bank Stadium again. "You know what, the reason is because the next thing on my mind is, as a team, we are poised to go do something. As men, we made a commitment to each other, and that is to head next week to Denver to get a win."

Flacco and the Ravens defense, which gave up plenty of yards but kept the Colts out of the end zone, turned a four-point halftime lead into a relatively comfortable victory, enabling the Ravens to pay tribute to Lewis in the game's final few minutes.

Shrugging off a sluggish start, Flacco threw second-half touchdown passes to tight end Dennis Pitta and wide receiver

Anquan Boldin as the Ravens pulled away from the Colts, who had rebounded from a two-win 2011 season to become one of the surprises of the NFL.

Held without a catch in the first half, Boldin set a team playoff record with 145 receiving yards on five catches. His 18-yard touchdown catch over Darius Butler with 9:14 to play gave the Ravens the 24-9 lead, and cornerback Cary Williams all but sealed the victory with an interception of rookie Andrew Luck on the Colts' next possession. The Ravens' 441 yards of offense, which included 103 rushing yards from rookie Bernard Pierce, were a franchise playoff record.

"The bottom line is, we haven't won it all, and that's been our goal, and that's our goal this year," Flacco said. "Right now we're just focused on going up to Denver, and we'll have to move on from this one quickly and get another step closer to our goal."

After the game, Boldin acknowledged that he wanted to play Denver again. When asked why Saturday will be different, the wide receiver said, "We'll make it different."

The AFC North champion Ravens entered the playoffs having lost four of five games. They showed significant progress in some areas while continuing to look vulnerable in others.

Quarterback Joe Flacco steps past linebacker Dwight Freeney to complete a 20-yard touchdown pass to tight end Dennis Pitta, giving the Ravens a 20-7 third-quarter lead. *Gene Sweeney Jr. | Baltimore Sun Photo*

Tight end Dennis Pitta drags Colts linebacker Moise Fokou (Maryland, Frostburg State) into the end zone for a 20-yard touchdown reception. *Gene Sweeney Jr. | Baltimore Sun Photo*

Running back Ray Rice shakes off Colts linebacker Jerrell Freeman in taking a short pass from Joe Flacco 47 yards to the Colts 2. The second-quarter play set up the go-ahead touchdown. *Lloyd Fox | Baltimore Sun Photo*

A retooled offensive line, which featured Bryant McKinnie at left tackle, Michael Oher at right tackle and Kelechi Osemele at left guard, allowed Flacco to be sacked only once and gave him the time to take several shots down the field. Flacco was 12-for-23 for 282 yards, two touchdowns and no turnovers in a game in which the Ravens averaged 7.9 yards per play and had eight plays of 20 yards or more.

The Ravens also rushed for 170 yards, but the ground game was marred by two fumbles by Ray Rice, his first two turnovers of the season.

"I'm going to address it. I'm not a fumbler, you guys know that, and that'll be the last time I address me fumbling," said Rice, who lost both fumbles in Colts territory. "It won't happen again."

On defense, the Ravens allowed the Colts to amass 419 yards and to control the ball for 37:32, but

they forced two turnovers and sacked Luck three times. Luck completed 28 of 54 passes for 288 yards but turned the ball over twice in Ravens territory.

By the time pregame introductions began, there wasn't an open seat to be found. After Ed Reed's name was announced — the safety also might have played his last home game as a Raven — Lewis came out and did his trademark dance as teammates rushed toward him. Flacco joked that he tried to persuade his wife, Dana, to bring in a video camera to capture the moment. Harbaugh also inched forward to get a good view.

With all the emotion on both sides — Colts head coach Chuck Pagano, a former Ravens defensive coordinator, was on the sideline for the second straight week after missing most of the season while being treated for leukemia — neither team got off to a particularly good start. The Ravens finally found the end zone on fullback Vonta Leach's 2-yard run 50 seconds before halftime, a score that was set up by a 47-yard screen pass to Rice.

That appeared to get Flacco going. He was 3-for-4 for 76 yards on the Ravens' second drive of the third quarter, which ended with a 20-yard touchdown to Pitta. After kicker

Adam Vinatieri's 40-yard miss early in the fourth, Flacco needed just five plays to get the Ravens into the end zone as he hit Boldin for 18 yards.

About an hour after the game and his victory lap, Lewis said he would allow his teammates to enjoy the victory for no more than 12 hours. Lewis had already turned in his iPad so it could be loaded with game film of Peyton Manning and the Broncos. Ravens fans might never forget Lewis' final home game, but the 37-year-old linebacker had already moved on.

"At the end of the day, it's not about me and Peyton. It's about their team against our team," Lewis said. "I just like our team. I love our team right now, and I'm really looking forward to going out there and playing them next week." ■

Linebacker Ray Lewis does a Cal Ripken Jr.-like victory lap around M&T Bank Stadium to salute the fans after his final home game.
Gene Sweeney Jr. | Baltimore Sun Photo

MIKE PRESTON'S REPORT CARD

QUARTERBACK — B-
Joe Flacco had a tough first half but played better in the second. Fortunately, the Ravens didn't have to count on him to make a lot of tight passes after halftime. He threw a lot of jump balls in the second half, and basically that was all that was needed.

RUNNING BACKS — B
Rookie Bernard Pierce had 103 rushing yards to top the 70 by Ray Rice. Rice fumbled twice to halt two drives but did have a 47-yard reception. Vonta Leach had a 1-yard touchdown run, and the Ravens used him in a short-yardage situation at the goal line.

RECEIVERS — C+
Anquan Boldin had the game receivers dream of, catching five passes for 145 yards. Tight end Dennis Pitta had two catches for 31 yards and a touchdown. The Ravens didn't have to throw a lot except to pick on cornerback Cassius Vaughn, who struggled.

OFFENSIVE LINE — B
This was a reshuffled group, but it's the unit the Ravens should have been starting weeks ago. The Ravens got strong performances from the left side — tackle Bryant McKinnie and guard Kelechi Osemele. Center Matt Birk got the group settled quickly with his calls.

DEFENSIVE LINE — C
The Colts had one of the worst rushing offenses in the NFL during the regular season, and running back Vick Ballard still ran for 91 yards on 22 carries. This group got little penetration and left the linebackers to clean up the mess.

LINEBACKERS — C+
Ray Lewis led the Ravens in tackles with 13 but showed the rust of not having played in about two months. Fellow inside linebacker Dannell Ellerbe had several big plays but missed easy tackles. Outside linebacker Paul Kruger was outstanding, with 2.5 sacks.

SECONDARY — C
Luck was betrayed by his receivers, who dropped a lot of passes and were intimidated by the Ravens, especially safety Bernard Pollard. The cornerbacks broke well on a lot of passes, but the Colts would have had a lot of open receivers if given time.

SPECIAL TEAMS — C+
Sam Koch rebounded from a poor performance a week ago and had a punt of 60 yards. Jacoby Jones returned a punt 34 yards and a kickoff 37 yards. Justin Tucker converted a 23-yard field goal, and the Ravens handled Indianapolis' return game well.

COACHING — C+
The Ravens finally made the necessary moves with the offensive line, but it shouldn't have taken that long. The Ravens went after the Colts' weakness on defense by throwing deep, but coordinator Dean Pees has to get stronger play from the defensive line.

SCORING SUMMARY

2nd Quarter
3:42   Bal   FG   Tucker 23
12:35 Ind   FG   Vinatieri 47
14:10 Bal   TD   Leach 2 run (Tucker kick)
15:00 Ind   FG   Vinatieri 52

3rd Quarter
6:34   Bal   TD   Pitta 20 pass from Flacco (Tucker kick)
14:20 Ind   FG   Vinatieri 26

4th Quarter
5:46   Bal   TD   Boldin 18 pass from Flacco (Tucker kick)

JANUARY 12, 2013	1	2	3	4	OT	OT	F
RAVENS	14	7	7	7	0	3	38
BRONCOS	14	7	7	7	0	0	35

IT'S A MILE HIGH MIRACLE

BY JEFF ZREBIEC, THE BALTIMORE SUN

Flacco's fling, Graham's picks, Tucker's kick in frigid temperatures make Ravens 'team of destiny'

DENVER — When the best game that almost every Ravens player had ever been a part of was finally over, Joe Flacco threw his hands in the air, Justin Tucker pumped his fist and Ray Lewis dropped to his knees, reduced to tears.

Tucker's 47-yard field goal 1 minute, 42 seconds into the second quarter of overtime ended a thrilling and exhausting divisional playoff game and sent the Ravens into the AFC championship game for the second straight year. The 38-35 victory over the Denver Broncos earned the Ravens a date with the winner of today's game between the New England Patriots and the Houston Texans. The AFC championship game will kick off next Sunday at 6:30 p.m. at the home of today's winner.

"When all the emotions calm down, it will probably be one of the greatest victories in Ravens history," said Lewis, whose retirement tour will extend at least one more week.

It also might be one of their most improbable victories. The

Jacoby Jones (12) is congratulated by fellow wide receiver Torrey Smith after tying the game at 35 with a 70-yard reception with 31 seconds remaining in regulation. *Lloyd Fox | Baltimore Sun Photo*

Ravens allowed two return touchdowns by Trindon Holliday, who became the first player in NFL history to accomplish that feat in the postseason, and they trailed by a touchdown with the ball at their 23 and 1:09 to go in regulation.

On third down from their 30, Flacco, who played one of his best games as a pro quarterback, spotted Jacoby Jones down the right sideline behind the Broncos defense and unleashed a pass that hung in the air seemingly forever.

Having beaten Tony Carter and Rahim Moore, Jones caught the ball and sprinted into the end zone with 31 seconds to play.

"I've never seen anything like that," said Ravens wide receiver Torrey Smith, who had two touchdown catches and outplayed Broncos star cornerback Champ Bailey. "You play some games on 'Madden' and you can't even do that."

The two teams traded punts to open overtime, but on the

Broncos' second possession, Peyton Manning threw across his body and was intercepted by cornerback Corey Graham, giving the Ravens the ball at the Denver 45. An 11-yard run by Ray Rice put Tucker in position to convert the game-winner.

"I always feel good about going out onto the field," said Tucker, a rookie free agent who beat out incumbent Billy Cundiff in training camp to win the kicking job. "Not a lot of people get to do this. This is a heck of a lot of fun."

The victory ended the top-seeded Broncos' 11-game winning streak and gave the Ravens their first back-to-back AFC championship game appearances in team history. They beat a Manning-quarterbacked team for just the third time in 12 tries and for

Rookie Justin Tucker punctuates the Ravens' victory after kicking the winning field goal from 47 yards 1:42 into the second quarter of overtime. Ed Dickson is at left. *Gene Sweeney Jr. | Baltimore Sun Photo*

Trindon Holliday outraces punter Sam Koch to score on a 90-yard return to give Denver a 7-0 lead in the first quarter. Holliday later returned a kickoff 104 yards. *Lloyd Fox | Baltimore Sun Photo*

BALTIMORE RAVENS

Wide receiver Anquan Boldin is tackled by Broncos safety Rahim Moore after a 19-yard reception in the fourth quarter took the ball to the Ravens 47. Boldin caught a pass for 17 yards on the next play. *Lloyd Fox | Baltimore Sun Photo*

the first time since the 2001 season.

It also provided an emphatic rebuttal to the Ravens' 34-17 home loss to the Broncos four weeks ago and to the questions all season that they were incapable of beating a good team on the road.

They certainly did that Saturday, overcoming four Broncos leads, Holliday's heroics, three touchdown passes by Manning, and temperatures that were below 10 degrees by game's end. It was the second-coldest game in Broncos history.

"I don't know if I'm amazed, but it was pretty incredible," Flacco said. "We overcame some things today, and we fought to the very end. Just like Tucker said and Ray said in the locker room, when some of those things did happen, none of us blinked. We just sat there on the sidelines and said, 'All right, our turn.' When some of those things did happen, no one worried. We just said, 'All right, our turn.' Slowly but surely, we were able to score points when we needed to, and our defense was able to stop them."

Protected well by an offensive line that played one of its best games of the season — tackles Bryant McKinnie and Michael Oher allowed just one total sack — Flacco completed 18 of 34 passes for 331 yards and three touchdowns.

"Maybe people will stop underestimating Joe finally," McKinnie said. "This could be the turning point in his career. People need to stop underestimating Joe and give him a little more respect."

Flacco hit Smith for touchdowns of 59 and 32 yards, the latter one tying the game at 21 heading into halftime. The teams combined for 28 points in the game's first 11 minutes, a torrid pace that started with Holliday's 90-yard punt-return touchdown and included Graham's 39-yard interception return for a touchdown.

Holliday started the second half with a 104-yard kickoff return that left the Ravens chasing a 28-21 deficit.

But Flacco, who shouldered a lot of blame for the Ravens' regular-season loss to the Broncos after his interception was returned 98 yards for a touchdown near the end of the first half, was hardly the only Raven to gain retribution. After fumbling twice in the Ravens' playoff-opening win over the Indianapolis Colts, Rice rushed 30 times for 131 yards and one touchdown. His 1-yard touchdown run with 20 seconds left in the third quarter tied the game at 28.

Manning's third touchdown of the day — a 17-yard pass to Demaryius Thomas — with just over 7 minutes to play capped a 10-play, 88-yard drive that broke a tie at 28. Thomas broke attempted tackles by Lewis and safety Ed Reed on the play.

Later, Flacco drove the Ravens to the Broncos 31. However, back-to-back drops — the first by Jones on third down and

Wide receiver Torrey Smith cuts inside Broncos corner-back Champ Bailey to catch a 32-yard pass to tie the game at 21 in the final minute of the second quarter. *Lloyd Fox | Baltimore Sun Photo*

Joe Flacco is pumped after his 59-yard scoring pass to wide receiver Torrey Smith tied the game at 7. Flacco completed 18 of 34 passes for 331 yards and three touchdowns.   *Lloyd Fox | Baltimore Sun Photo*

BALTIMORE RAVENS

Linebacker Ray Lewis and defensive end Pernell McPhee (90) celebrate a third-quarter fumble recovery.
Lloyd Fox | Baltimore Sun Photo

the second by tight end Dennis Pitta on fourth down — turned the ball over on downs. The Ravens eventually forced the Broncos to punt, but they were 77 yards from the end zone with no timeouts and just over a minute to play.

Enter Jones.

"I told myself that Joe might throw me the ball, so I'd better haul butt off the line," Jones said.

After the game was over, Rice declared the Ravens "the team of destiny."

"Just think about it," he said. "You give up two special teams touchdowns and the way Peyton played, odds say we're going to lose, but I think we're the only group of people ... that believed that we could get it done, and we did it."

Ravens coach John Harbaugh will be in his third

Cornerback Corey Graham puts the Ravens up 14-7 in the first quarter with a 39-yard interception return of a pass by Denver's Peyton Manning. Graham later intercepted Manning in overtime to set up the winning field goal. *Gene Sweeney Jr.* | *Baltimore Sun Photo*

Running back Ray Rice gives a Mile High salute after his 1-yard run tied the game at 28. *Lloyd Fox | Baltimore Sun Photo*

Linebacker Ray Lewis celebrates the victory, which extended his NFL career at least one week and put the Ravens into the AFC championship game for the third time in five seasons. *Lloyd Fox | Baltimore Sun Photo*

AFC championship game in five seasons, and while he abhors comparisons, it's hard to imagine a more rewarding trip than this.

"That was one of the best football games you're ever going to see," Harbaugh said. "That football game did the game of football proud. I'm just proud and grateful to have an opportunity to be part of this game. ... Our guys did not crack."

As a result, the Ravens boarded a plane Saturday evening for a long trip home, knowing they still have more football to play.

"It was amazing. All the crazy stuff that went on — a punt return, a kick return — nobody flinched, man," safety Bernard Pollard said. "Everybody stayed the path, and that was good for us. We're excited not to be packing our locker room up and going home." ■

MIKE PRESTON'S REPORT CARD

QUARTERBACK — A
Joe Flacco threw some excellent passes and handled pressure in the pocket well. The two touchdown passes to Torrey Smith were placed perfectly, and that heave to Jacoby Jones in the final seconds was more than Denver expected.

RUNNING BACKS — B-
Neither Ray Rice nor Bernard Pierce was dominant, but they were steady and wore down Denver in the final quarter. Rice was strong in the third quarter and tough on the goal line. On some runs, they made yardage without holes.

RECEIVERS — A
Smith had two touchdown catches, and he simply outran Champ Bailey on both. Jones had only one reception, but it was the biggest of the game. Tight end Dennis Pitta came through in several clutch situations. Receivers don't come any tougher than Anquan Boldin.

OFFENSIVE LINE — B
The Ravens were solid in the running game and strong against the best pass-rushing group in the NFL. The Ravens didn't allow a sack until late in the game, and Flacco was hit only once. Flacco did a nice job of stepping up in the pocket.

DEFENSIVE LINE — C
Defensive tackles Haloti Ngata and Ma'ake Kemoeatu were solid in the middle, and the Ravens used a strong rotation to stay fresh. This group could have put more pressure on quarterback Peyton Manning.

LINEBACKERS — C
The Ravens had a lot of tackles, but most of those came down the field. The Ravens weren't very good in pass coverage, but they did get a strong performance from inside linebacker Dannell Ellerbe. Outside linebacker Terrell Suggs wasn't consistent but did have several big plays.

SECONDARY — C
This wasn't a great performance by the secondary, but it was an upgrade from a week ago. The Ravens started slowly but got better as the game went on and actually started jumping some pass routes. The Ravens became more aggressive as the game progressed.

SPECIAL TEAMS — F
The Ravens allowed a kick return of 104 yards for a touchdown and a punt return 90 yards for a touchdown. That's unacceptable.

COACHING — B
The Ravens took advantage of the mismatch with Bailey and stayed after him. For the most part, the Ravens handled Manning and didn't allow him to control the game. Special teams were a disaster.

SCORING SUMMARY

1st Quarter

2:46	Den	TD	Holliday 90 punt return (Prater kick)
4:29	Bal	TD	T. Smith 59 pass from Flacco (Tucker kick)
5:11	Bal	TD	Graham 39 int. return (Tucker kick)
10:58	Den	TD	Stokley 15 pass from Manning (Prater kick)

2nd Quarter

7:34	Den	TD	Moreno 14 pass from Manning (Prater kick)
14:24	Bal	TD	T. Smith 32 pass from Flacco (Tucker kick)

3rd Quarter

0:13	Den	TD	Holliday 104 kickoff return (Prater kick)
14:40	Bal	TD	Rice 1 run (Tucker kick)

4th Quarter

7:49	Den	TD	Thomas 17 pass from Manning (Prater kick)
14:29	Bal	TD	J. Jones 70 pass from Flacco (Tucker kick)

2nd Overtime

1:42	Bal	FG	Tucker 47

JANUARY 20, 2013	1	2	3	4	F
RAVENS	0	7	7	14	28
PATRIOTS	3	10	0	0	13

A STUNNING SECOND ACT

BY JEFF ZREBIEC, THE BALTIMORE SUN

Ravens hold Patriots scoreless after half-time, put together three touchdown drives to avenge last year's bitter defeat

FOXBOROUGH, Mass. — They wanted the New England Patriots, told the world they would beat them and then went into their stadium and dominated the second half as no visiting team had ever done.

It didn't seem possible when they limped into the postseason as losers in four of their past five, or when they trailed the Denver Broncos last week by a touchdown with under a minute to go, or during Sunday night's first half, when they were having trouble getting quarterback Tom Brady off the field.

But it's reality now: The Ravens are going to the Super Bowl. Avenging last year's bitter loss to the Patriots in the AFC championship game, the Ravens took apart New England in the second half, punching their ticket to New Orleans with a thorough 28-13 victory in front of an announced 68,756 at stunned Gillette Stadium.

"We know what it felt like walking off that field losers" last season, Ravens safety Bernard

Linebacker Terrell Suggs poses in Ravens Country. "We came, we saw and we conquered," Suggs said after the game.   *Lloyd Fox | Baltimore Sun Photo*

Pollard said. "They beat us, and we said we weren't going to walk off again like that."

Instead, the Ravens bounced off, one by one, celebrating with the team's fans, who had come down to the first couple of rows at Gillette Stadium. Safety Ed Reed, who will play in his first Super Bowl and do it in his home state, sang, "We got two tickets to paradise." Outside linebacker Terrell Suggs yelled, "We came, we saw and we conquered." Defensive end Arthur Jones held up a sign that read "AFC champions"

and shouted to no one in particular, "Hallelujah, Hallelujah."

In the Super Bowl for the second time in team history and the first time in 12 years, the Ravens will play the San Francisco 49ers, 28-24 winners over the Atlanta Falcons in the NFC championship game, on Feb. 3 at the Mercedes-Benz Superdome. The game will pit Ravens coach John Harbaugh against his younger brother, Jim, the coach of the 49ers.

"I don't know if we had a

Fans gather after the game in the 1100 block of South Charles Street, as seen from the roof of Mother's Federal Hill Grille.
Algerina Perna | Baltimore Sun Photo

dream this big," John Harbaugh said. "We had a few dreams, we had a few fights, we had a few arguments. We'll try to stay out of that business. We'll let the two teams duke it out."

John Harbaugh's team was at its best when it absolutely had to be, steamrollering Bill Belichick's Patriots — who led 13-7 at halftime — over the final 30 minutes. Belichick had been 72-1 when leading at halftime at Gillette Stadium, including 67-0 with Brady at the helm. But they

had no answers for quarterback Joe Flacco or for a Ravens defense that not only forced three turnovers in the second half, but also forced several Patriots to the sideline.

"We felt like the most physical team was going to win," Ravens wide receiver Anquan Boldin said. "I don't know if they know it or not, but the Ravens are a physical team. That's just the way we play, like it or not, offensively or defensively. If you think you're going to come in

here and knock us around, you have another think coming."

A week after outshining the Denver Broncos' Peyton Manning and two weeks after getting the better of Indianapolis Colts phenom Andrew Luck, Flacco outplayed Brady, completing 15 of 24 passes in the second half for 159 yards and three touchdowns after the coaching staff decided in the third quarter to put the game on the fifth-year quarterback's shoulders.

Defensive tackle Haloti Ngata (92) and linebacker Ray Lewis stop Patriots running back Shane Vereen for a 1-yard gain in the first quarter. *Gene Sweeney Jr.* | *Baltimore Sun Photo*

Wide receiver Anquan Boldin outleaps Patriots safety Devin McCourty for a 3-yard touchdown reception that put the Ravens up 21-13 in the fourth quarter. Boldin scored again less than 4 minutes later. *Kenneth K. Lam | Baltimore Sun Photo*

2013 SUPER BOWL CHAMPIONS

Running back Ray Rice cuts between Patriots safety Devin McCourty and linebacker Jerod Mayo to score from 2 yards out, putting the Ravens up 7-3 in the second quarter. Rice carried 19 times for 48 yards. *Lloyd Fox | Baltimore Sun Photo*

"We realized we needed to put some pressure on them," said Flacco, who has thrown eight touchdown passes and no interceptions in three playoff games this year. "We didn't come all the way here to play it safe."

With his team still trailing by six points about midway through the third quarter, Flacco hit tight end Dennis Pitta for a 5-yard touchdown that gave the Ravens a 14-13 lead they never relinquished. On the first play of the fourth quarter, he found Boldin for a 3-yard score, and a little more than three minutes later, the pair connected for an 11-yard touchdown. Boldin had said during the week that the Ravens would win, and his two touchdowns made sure of that.

"For us, it wasn't a secret what we were trying to accomplish," Boldin said. "We came here last year and we left with a bitter taste in our mouths. We felt like this team took something

Pressured by defensive tackle Haloti Ngata, Patriots quarterback Tom Brady throws an incompletion. Brady was 29-for-54 for 320 yards, one touchdown and two interceptions. *Kenneth K. Lam | Baltimore Sun Photo*

Joyful coach John Harbaugh redirects attention to quarterback Joe Flacco, who completed 21 of 36 passes for 240 yards and three touchdowns in outplaying Tom Brady in the AFC championship game for a second straight year. *Gene Sweeney Jr.* **| Baltimore Sun Photo**

away from us. We wanted to come back and make that right. It would have been great to do it in front of our fans in Baltimore at M&T Bank Stadium, but we thought the proper way was to come back here and to win at Foxborough, and we were able to do that."

Leading 28-13 with 11:13 to play, the Ravens stopped the Patriots on fourth down to get the ball back, then got interceptions on New England's final two possessions. Brady finished 29-for-54 for 320 yards, one touchdown and two interceptions.

"It's our time. It's our time," said Ravens inside linebacker Ray Lewis, whose retirement tour will go right down to the season's final day in New Orleans. "Every man out there sacrificed this year for each other. And we did it, we did it, we did it. We're on our way to the Super Bowl. That's awesome."

Lewis, who announced a couple of days before the playoff opener that this would be his "final ride," dropped to his knees on the field after the clock hit zero. Individual cele-

Linebacker Ray Lewis, with guard Bobbie Williams, exults in the Ravens' championship-game victory and his second trip to the Super Bowl. *Lloyd Fox* **| Baltimore Sun Photo**

brations popped up everywhere while Flacco held the ball aloft. It was a scene that would few would have expected about a month ago.

"It's who we are," said Ravens wide receiver Torrey Smith (Maryland), who caught four passes for 69 yards. "That's what our city is, a tough city. You get knocked down, you've got to get back up. That's how life is. You just can't lay down and roll over. You've got to continue to fight."

Trailing 13-7 in the third quarter, the Ravens caught a break when Wes Welker dropped an easy pass from Brady that would, at the very least, have put New England in field-goal position to take a two-possession lead. The Patriots punted instead and would never score again, nor would they stop Flacco when they needed to.

Taking over at his 13, Flacco put together his sharpest drive of the game. He hit Pitta to get the ball to midfield. Ray Rice then turned a dump-off into a 15-yard gain. An 8-yard run by rookie Bernard Pierce picked up another first down, and then Flacco hit Boldin for 12 yards. On the next play, after Pitta was drilled by Jerod Mayo following a 5-yard completion, the tight end shook free from safety Steve Gregory for a 5-yard touchdown catch.

On the drive, which covered 87 plays on 10 plays, Flacco, who had completed just six of 12 passes for 81 yards in the first half, was 6-for-9 for 64 yards — and he was just getting warmed up.

After the defense gave the Ravens the ball right back, Flacco hit Smith for 23 yards. Pierce had two runs for 17 yards to get the Ravens inside the Patriots 20. From there,

Safety Ed Reed can't hold back the tears after the Ravens defeated the Patriots. He's holding a Baltimore Sun celebratory page. *Lloyd Fox | Baltimore Sun Photo*

Flacco hit Pitta for 6 yards and Boldin for 8. On second-and-goal from the 3, Flacco lofted a pass to Boldin, who outleaped Devin McCourty for a touchdown. That gave the Ravens a 21-13 lead with under 5 minutes to go in the third.

On the Patriots' next possession, a thunderous hit by Pollard on Stevan Ridley, which Harbaugh called the play of the game, caused a fumble and knocked the Patriots running back from the game. Jones re-

Coach John Harbaugh is sprayed with sparkling wine in the locker room after the Ravens defeated the Patriots for their second AFC championship.
Kenneth K. Lam | Baltimore Sun Photo

QUARTERBACK — A
Despite his receivers dropping passes early, Joe Flacco showed no frustration and ripped into the Patriots in the third quarter, completing 11 of 18 passes. The back-shoulder throw to receiver Anquan Boldin early in the fourth quarter was a beauty.

RUNNING BACKS — C+
Starter Ray Rice began slowly, but he made some big plays as a runner and receiver. The Ravens got a lot of juice from backup Bernard Pierce and his downhill running ability. They didn't have big numbers but were solid.

RECEIVERS — B
Coordinator Jim Caldwell opened up the offense in the second half and started taking more chances with Boldin and Torrey Smith. The Patriots had no answer for Boldin in the second half, but this team needs to work on comeback routes. Tight end Dennis Pitta had some clutch receptions, too.

OFFENSIVE LINE — A
This group has been outstanding ever since veteran Bryant McKinnie was inserted back as the starting left tackle. Right guard Marshal Yanda was outstanding and wears down opponents. Center Matt Birk did a nice job when the Patriots went to a four-man front.

DEFENSIVE LINE — C+
The Patriots had a lot of yardage, but the Ravens prevented big plays. The Ravens shuffled a lot of players and were prepared for New England's no-huddle attack. Tackle Haloti Ngata had two quarterback pressures.

LINEBACKERS — C
Outside linebacker Terrell Suggs had a solid game, and so did inside linebacker Dannell Ellerbe. Ray Lewis had a lot of tackles but got pushed around the field a lot. Outside linebacker-end Paul Kruger got bounced around a lot.

SECONDARY — B-
The cornerbacks struggled with the Patriots' short passing game, but they kept New England from gaining a lot of yards after the catch. Free safety Ed Reed wasn't much of a factor, but strong safety Bernard Pollard had a physical presence. Overall, it was a good effort against a quality quarterback.

SPECIAL TEAMS — B
The Ravens had problems with Wes Welker on punt returns, but they stayed in their lanes on kick coverage. The Ravens have to get better play from special teams ace Brendon Ayanbadejo. Punter Sam Koch hasn't had a real strong postseason.

COACHING — A
Offensively, the Ravens were conservative in the first half, but Caldwell opened it up in the second. Defensively, the Ravens gave up a lot of yards but not a lot of points. For the second straight week, they went on the road as underdogs and won.

SCORING SUMMARY

1st Quarter
8:39 NE FG Gostkowski 31

2nd Quarter
5:32 Bal TD Rice 2 run (Tucker kick)
10:42 NE TD Welker 1 pass from Brady (Gostkowski kick)
15:00 NE FG Gostkowski 25

3rd Quarter
8:46 Bal TD Pitta 5 pass from Flacco (Tucker kick)

4th Quarter
0:04 Bal TD Boldin 3 pass from Flacco (Tucker kick)
3:47 Bal TD Boldin 11 pass from Flacco (Tucker kick)

covered, and the Ravens needed just four plays to get back into the end zone.

Flacco hit Smith for 16 yards, ran for 14 yards, connected with Jacoby Jones for 6 yards and threw a beautiful back-shoulder pass to Boldin that beat safety Devin McCourty for an 11-yard touchdown. The score gave the Ravens a 28-13 lead with 11:13 to play and left Gillette Stadium shocked.

"The guys came out in the second half and made plays," Flacco said. "We were able to go up and down the field a handful of consecutive times and score points, and that's what we needed to do against this football team. We needed to put pressure on them like that, and it worked pretty well."

The last couple of minutes essentially morphed into a conference coronation for the Ravens. Flacco playfully shoved Harbaugh a couple of times before the coach finally pushed him back. Owner Steve Bisciotti came down to the sideline and embraced Lewis. Flacco initially asked his teammates to settle down on the sideline because there was still time on the clock for Brady.

But there was no stopping the Ravens on this night. It seemed improbable not too long ago, but there was little doubt in the second half Sunday night. Next stop: New Orleans.

"I have no words, man," Reed said. "I'm just grateful for our coaches. For everything we've been through since Coach Harbaugh got here, he had a vision of working us a certain way and taking us through something to build and to create this moment. We believed it, but it was just something we had to go through as men and understand each other and understand the process together." ■

FEBRUARY 3, 2013	1	2	3	4	F
RAVENS	7	14	7	6	34
49ERS	3	3	17	8	31

SURGE PROTECTORS

BY JEFF ZREBIEC, THE BALTIMORE SUN

After early dominance and electrical outage, Ravens hold on to bring home second championship

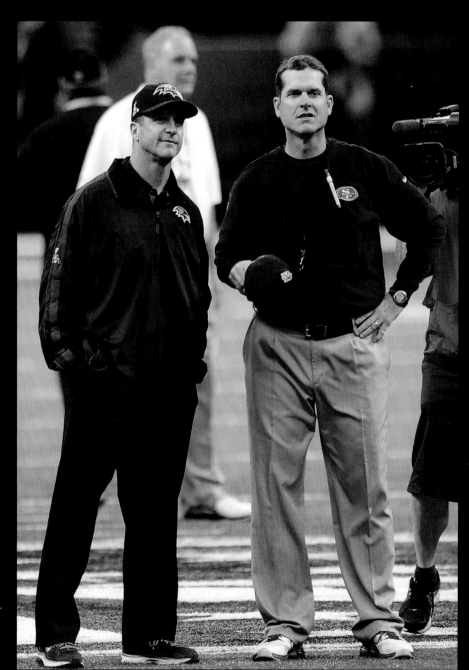

NEW ORLEANS — Ray Lewis' last ride has ended with a Ravens coronation, and the grand vision he has shared with teammates for more than a decade is now fulfilled.

Twelve years after they won their first Super Bowl with Lewis and the defense leading the way, the Ravens reigned again Sunday night, finishing off a surprising playoff run with a thrilling 34-31 victory over the San Francisco 49ers in Super Bowl XLVII at the Mercedes-Benz Superdome.

Behind the arm of Joe Flacco, the legs of Jacoby Jones and a defense that stiffened at the most crucial time, the Ravens survived a frantic comeback to send Lewis out on top and give coach John Harbaugh bragging rights over his younger brother, Jim, coach of the 49ers.

When the two brothers met at midfield after the game, John said, he told Jim that he loved him.

Coach John Harbaugh, left, stands with his brother, 49ers coach Jim Harbaugh, on the field before the game.
Kenneth K. Lam | Baltimore Sun Photo

Ravens players, including punter Sam Koch (4), linebacker Brendon Ayanbadejo (51) and defensive back James Ihedigbo (32), take the field at the start of the Super Bowl. *Lloyd Fox | Baltimore Sun Photo*

"It wasn't pretty, it wasn't perfect, but it was us," said John Harbaugh, who took the Lombardi Trophy from owner Steve Bisciotti and held it aloft. "The final series of Ray Lewis' career was a goal-line stand to win the Lombardi Trophy. As Ray said on the podium, how could it be any better than that?"

But it wasn't easy, especially after a 34-minute power outage in the Superdome cost the Ravens the momentum they had gained from a dominant first half and Jones' 108-yard kickoff return to start the second. After the stoppage in the third quarter, the 49ers scored 17 straight points to cut the Ravens' lead to 28-23.

"I just knew that with Jim Harbaugh on the other sideline and all those years being together, that those guys were going to come back," John Harbaugh said. "Those guys handled [the delay] better than we did."

Before the darkness, the game was Flacco's. Completing one of the best postseasons by a quarterback, Flacco threw three touchdown passes — all in the first half — to capture the Super Bowl Most Valuable Player award and, perhaps, quiet his skeptics for good. Jones, who caught one of those scoring passes, gave the Ravens a 28-6 lead before the power cut out.

But fittingly, after a season in which they battled inconsistency, injuries and tragedy, the Ravens needed one last defensive stand.

Wide receiver Anquan Boldin catches a 13-yard touchdown pass from Joe Flacco. The score gave the Ravens a 7-0 lead less than five minutes into the game.
Gene Sweeney Jr. | Baltimore Sun Photo

Nose tackle Terrence Cody (62) pressures 49ers quarterback Colin Kaepernick in the first quarter. Cody finished with one assisted tackle in the game. *Gene Sweeney Jr.* | *Baltimore Sun Photo*

Quarterback Colin Kaepernick, whose comeback efforts helped San Francisco to three second-half touchdowns and a field goal, moved the 49ers down to the Ravens 5-yard line with two minutes to go. That was as far as they got. Three straight incompletions, the final one just eluding the grasp of wide receiver Michael Crabtree, gave the Ravens the ball back.

Less than two minutes later, after Josh Bynes pulled down Ted Ginn Jr. at midfield on a game-ending free-kick return, the Ravens burst toward the middle of the field to celebrate. A pile of players materialized near midfield as purple confetti rained down on them. Other players made snow angels as a pro-Ravens crowd, which had sweated through the final minutes of the 49ers' comeback attempt, erupted.

It was exactly the scene that Lewis had told his teammates about for so many years.

"We finished it. It just shows what our team was built for. We were here to finish this race, and we finished it," Lewis said. "I wanted to see their faces when that confetti came out of the sky.

... That's the greatest reward as a leader, to talk to them about a vision and then finishing it. To bring Baltimore a second ring before I hang up my cleats, there's just no better way to go out."

Now Lewis — the only remaining player from the team that blitzed the New York Giants to win Super Bowl XXXV — and his teammates will get one more ride: a trip through the streets of downtown Baltimore for a parade Tuesday morning.

It was Ozzie Newsome's second title, further solidifying him as one of the game's best general managers. Still, the team's top executives had said all week that this was about the players, and nobody enjoyed the victory more than safety Ed Reed, who had played 11 years to get this opportunity.

After the victory here, less than a half-hour from his hometown of Saint Rose, Reed went from sideline to sideline, whooping it up with fans. He called the victory a microcosm of the Ravens' season.

"Started good, got ugly, ended great," said Reed, who had an interception in the game.

Then there was Flacco, who completed a near-perfect postseason — in four games, he had 11 touchdown passes and no interceptions — by completing 22 of 33 throws for 287 yards and three touchdowns. When the 49ers cut the Ravens' once-comfortable lead to 28-23 after scores on three straight possessions, Flacco answered with a drive that resulted in a 19-yard field goal by Justin Tucker.

After a 15-yard touchdown run by Kaepernick and a failed 2-point conversion left the Ravens with a 31-29 advantage with almost 10 minutes left, Flacco engineered another march, this one again ending on a field goal by Tucker with 4 minutes, 19 seconds to play. Flacco then went to the sideline and, like everybody else in purple, held his breath as the Ravens defense, the second-most effective red-zone unit during the regular season, held San Francisco out of the end zone.

Flacco threw three first-half touchdown passes — a 13-yarder to wide receiver Anquan Boldin on the Ravens' first drive, a 1-yard connection with tight end Dennis Pitta to make it 14-3 and then a 56-yard strike to Jones for a 21-3 lead. Jones had come back for the deep ball, tumbled to the turf on the catch and then, seeing he was untouched, got up and ran into the

Running back Bernard Pierce is brought down by 49ers safety Dashon Goldson in the third quarter. Pierce rushed 12 times for 33 yards in the game.
Lloyd Fox | Baltimore Sun Photo

2013 SUPER BOWL CHAMPIONS

Safety Ed Reed intercepts a second-quarter pass from the 49ers' Colin Kaepernick. The Ravens couldn't score on the ensuing possession. *Gene Sweeney Jr.* | *Baltimore Sun Photo*

Quarterback Joe Flacco runs onto the field as time expires. The Super Bowl's Most Valuable Player completed 22 of 33 passes for 287 yards and three touchdowns, with no interceptions.   *Kenneth K. Lam | Baltimore Sun Photo*

Tight end Dennis Pitta, left, and linebacker Ray Lewis share a moment after their 34-31 victory over the 49ers.
Lloyd Fox | Baltimore Sun Photo

Coach John Harbaugh, left, and team owner Steve Bisciotti hug after the Ravens' 34-31 victory. *Lloyd Fox | Baltimore Sun Photo*

QUARTERBACK — A

Joe Flacco continued his hot streak and playoff dominance. His consistency has improved with his mechanics, and he appears to have more pocket awareness. There were several times when he stepped up in the pocket to make big plays, something he hadn't done earlier.

RUNNING BACKS — C+

This group appeared to be in slow-motion at times, and fullback Vonta Leach was often late finding the 49ers inside linebackers. Ray Rice tiptoed at the line of scrimmage in the first half while backup Bernard Pierce attacked it. The Ravens should have played Pierce more.

RECEIVERS — B

San Francisco cornerbacks feared the Ravens' big-play ability and provided a big cushion. Anquan Boldin worked the intermediate and short stuff, and tight ends Dennis Pitta and Ed Dickson were open constantly. Boldin, though, dropped three passes.

OFFENSIVE LINE — B

The Ravens dominated the 49ers up front in the first half, and they often ran left, behind tackle Bryant McKinnie and guard Kelechi Osemele. Right guard Marshal Yanda and Osemele did a nice job of getting to the 49ers inside linebackers. Center Matt Birk was solid as usual.

DEFENSIVE LINE — B-

The Ravens were tough up front and weren't confused by the pistol offense. Tackles Haloti Ngata and Ma'ake Kemoeatu held their own against double teams. Arthur Jones was outstanding, but the Ravens didn't get much of an inside rush except for Jones.

LINEBACKERS — C

Outside linebackers Paul Kruger and Terrell Suggs got pressure, and inside linebacker Dannell Ellerbe was outstanding, especially in the first half. The Ravens had trouble covering tight end Vernon Davis across the field, and sometimes this group had shallow drops.

SECONDARY — C

This unit did a good job in the first half of blanketing some of the NFL's best receivers, who seldom got open downfield. Cornerback Cary Williams broke on the ball well, and safety Ed Reed had an interception. Receiver Randy Moss acted as if he didn't want to be in the game.

SPECIAL TEAMS — B-

The coverage units did a decent job except for a punt return by Ted Ginn Jr. in the third quarter. Jacoby Jones returned a kickoff for a touchdown. Punter Sam Koch struggled at times, as he did for most of the postseason.

COACHING — B

John Harbaugh handled his team well all week and had the players ready. The decision to fake the field goal was stunningly stupid. Offensively, the Ravens played well and kept the 49ers off balance. Defensively, they gave up too much yardage in the second half.

SCORING SUMMARY

1st Quarter

4:24	Bal	TD	Boldin 13 pass from Flacco (Tucker kick)
11:02	SF	FG	Akers 36

2nd Quarter

7:50	Bal	TD	Pitta 1 pass from Flacco (Tucker kick)
13:15	Bal	TD	J. Jones 56 pass from Flacco (Tucker kick)
15:00	SF	FG	Akers 27

3rd Quarter

0:11	Bal	TD	J. Jones 108 kickoff return (Tucker kick)
7:40	SF	TD	Crabtree 31 pass from Kaepernick (Akers kick)
10:01	SF	TD	Gore 6 run (Akers kick)
11:50	SF	FG	Akers 34

4th Quarter

2:06	Bal	FG	Tucker 19
5:03	SF	TD	Kaepernick 15 run (pass failed)
10:41	Bal	FG	Tucker 38
14:56	SF	SAF	Koch forced out of bounds in end zone

end zone. The touchdown tied Flacco with Joe Montana and Kurt Warner for the most in a postseason.

When Jones burst through the middle and returned the opening kickoff of the second half for a 108-yard touchdown and a 28-6 margin, the Ravens appeared well on their way to a second title. There were still nearly 30 minutes left to play, but to that point, the Ravens had dominated in every way.

A 31-yard touchdown pass from Kaepernick to Crabtree, who spun off cornerback Cary Williams and strong safety Bernard Pollard, made it 28-13. A little more than two minutes later, it was 28-20 after a long punt return from Ginn set up a 6-yard rushing touchdown by running back Frank Gore.

It would get worse. Running back Ray Rice fumbled in

Ravens territory, and Chykie Brown's roughing-the-kicker penalty gave David Akers a second chance. He converted from 34 yards, and the lead was down to five.

But as they have all season, the Ravens answered the 49ers at every turn until, at last, their ride was finished.

"At no point in the game did we think that we were going to lose," said linebacker Terrell Suggs, who had played 10 seasons before winning his first title. "As long as we had the lead, we knew we had them. They can call us whatever we want, but they've got to put champions on it. The Baltimore Ravens are world champions, baby." ∎

NOBODY THOUGHT THEY COULD DO IT

BY MIKE PRESTON, THE BALTIMORE SUN

The Ravens were underdogs in their last three postseason games but thrived in that role

There's no mistaking which team Cindy Pierce of Severn is rooting for as she shows off her purple wig and super boa outside the Mercedes-Benz Superdome in New Orleans. *Lloyd Fox | Baltimore Sun Photo*

NEW ORLEANS — There are always Cinderella stories in sports, but the Ravens' improbable journey to the Super Bowl XLVII championship is one of the best stories in recent football history.

A lot of the preseason experts picked the Ravens to win the AFC North, but few chose them to win their second Lombardi Trophy in 13 seasons. The Ravens had to hang on to win against a stubborn San Francisco 49ers team, 34-31, Sunday night before a sellout crowd at the Mercedes-Benz Superdome. What did you expect?

The only thing better might have been quarterback Joe Flacco throwing a 70-yard touchdown pass in the closing seconds of regulation in the divisional playoff game against the Denver Broncos.

"The win was representative and symbolic of our city," Flacco said. "We're a blue-collar city, and all our games end up like this. I knew San Francisco was going to come back, and I knew we had to keep grinding it out."

"We said, 'Stay buckled up, Baltimore' and we did," safety Ed Reed said.

Name a team that has come as far in one season. The Indianapolis Colts in 2007? The Pittsburgh Steelers in 2009? The New York Giants last year? Not one of them.

So, maybe that's why cornerback Chykie Brown was making snow angels in the confetti on the field Sunday night and why Reed tried to get Ray Lewis to do his "Squirrel Dance" in the end zone in the final minutes.

"My teammates, what we believed in from Day One is the most ultimate feeling," Lewis said. "This is the greatest feeling ever."

It was a dream run through the postseason, in which the Ravens were heavy underdogs on the road in the divisional playoffs against Denver, then had to travel to New England, where only a year before, their season ended in frustration in a loss to the Patriots in the AFC championship game. They won that game, too.

It was different here Sunday night. As the Ravens ran around the stadium, they were showered by thousands of Baltimore fans who made the trip and filled nearly three-quarters of the stadium. It had the flavor of a game at M&T Bank Stadium.

It was a special weekend for the Ravens. They had the first player drafted in franchise history, Jonathan Ogden, selected to the Pro Football Hall of Fame, and the face of the franchise since it moved to Baltimore, Ray Lewis, end his illustrious 17-year career with the title.

Quarterback Joe Flacco lets fly with a pass to tight end Dennis Pitta in the second quarter. Pitta had four receptions for 26 yards and a touchdown in the game. *Gene Sweeney Jr.* | *Baltimore Sun Photo*

And the night ended in redemption for the often-maligned Flacco, the Super Bowl Most Valuable Player, who completed 22 of 33 passes for 287 yards and three touchdowns. Flacco's passing numbers for the postseason were 73-for-126 for 1,140 yards, 11 touchdowns and no interceptions. The 1,140 passing yards are third most by a quarterback in a postseason.

No one predicted that one, either. In retrospect, this was almost supposed to be a rebuilding year for the Ravens. They lost good veteran players such as outside linebacker Jarret Johnson and defensive end Cory Redding.

Their best pass rusher and reigning NFL Defensive Player of the Year, Terrell Suggs, tore his Achilles tendon during the summer and missed almost half the season. By the time Suggs returned, the Ravens were faced with losing Lewis, who tore a triceps and missed the second half of the season.

At the same time, the Ravens were having a youth movement on defense with Arthur Jones, Paul Kruger, Albert McClellan and Courtney Upshaw working with new defensive coordinator Dean Pees.

Nobody thought this team was going far in the postseason, not even the Ravens.

"It means the world. All the stuff we've been through, this is what it is all about," Jones said. "Staying together as a team. Oh, my God, it feels so good."

The Ravens had problems on offense, as well. Flacco was strong early in the season but struggled after the midway point when the Ravens lost three of four games. After losing to the Pittsburgh Steelers and Washington Redskins in back-to-back weeks, the Ravens fired offensive coordinator Cam Cameron and replaced him with Jim Caldwell.

Super Bowl teams don't do that. Losing teams pull those kinds of moves. It was different with the Ravens. Flacco got better, and so did the offensive line as coach John

Running back Ray Rice leaps to gain 7 yards on a second-quarter rush. Rice carried 20 times for 59 yards in the game. *Lloyd Fox | Baltimore Sun Photo*

Harbaugh released left tackle Bryant McKinnie from the doghouse and put him into the starting lineup because of a toe injury to left guard Jah Reid.

If Reid doesn't get hurt, then McKinnie likely doesn't play. If McKinnie doesn't play, this team doesn't get to "The Show." It's weird, of course, but it's all part of the improbable journey.

"It is all part of a successful season, we've been through these things before and if we continue to work, it will work out," Flacco said. "Sometimes we have failed, but most of the time we have won."

They did again Sunday night.■

All eyes are on Jacoby Jones (12) after the Pro Bowl return man ran back a kickoff 108 yards to open the second half.
Kenneth K. Lam | Baltimore Sun Photo

AFTER FLICKER OF DOUBT, SHINING BRIGHTLY

BY PETER SCHMUCK, THE BALTIMORE SUN

Power outage and 49ers rally were the last obstacles the Ravens needed to overcome

Ravens fans pour onto South Charles Street in Baltimore's Federal Hill neighborhood to celebrate the team's second Super Bowl championship.
Amy Davis | Baltimore Sun Photo

NEW ORLEANS — Chalk it up to the "Ray Lewis Effect" if you want. Call it destiny or some other overused term for that which defies logical explanation. The only thing that matters now is that you can call the Ravens the undisputed champions of the football world.

The journey everybody has been talking about in the Ravens locker room for the last month officially came to an end at 10:44 p.m. Sunday with their arrival at the mountaintop. Three straight times, the oddsmakers said it couldn't be done only to have newly minted Super Bowl Most Valuable Player Joe Flacco and the Ravens prove them wrong every time, finishing with a 34-31 victory over the San Francisco 49ers.

What exactly did you expect to happen when they got to the Big Easy and everything they had worked so long and hard for was finally within reach?

Did you really think Flacco was suddenly going to stop piling up playoff touchdown passes when he got to the Mercedes-Benz Superdome?

Did you seriously believe that Lewis would play the last game of his terrific 17-year career and walk off the field with the same number of championship rings he

came with?

"How else do you say 'thank you' to your teammates and the people of Baltimore who believed in you?" Lewis said. "We're going to take the trophy back to them. There's just no better way to go out."

Of course, Lewis couldn't have stayed out of the spotlight if he had tried, but this night belonged to Joe Cool, who has spent this postseason setting records and poking a football in the face of everyone who ever questioned whether he belonged among the NFL's elite quarterbacks.

That conversation should have ended when he dispensed with Peyton Manning and Tom Brady in

the previous two playoff rounds, but it was Super Bowl week, and he had to answer the "elite" question only about a hundred times. It doesn't have to be asked ever again.

Flacco threw for three touchdowns in the first half and Jacoby Jones seemed to put the final nail in the 49ers with a 108-yard touchdown return to open the second half, but nothing has ever come that easily for this Ravens team.

Moments after Justin Tucker kicked the extra point and put the Ravens up by 22 points, the cranky electrical system in the Superdome decided the plot line for the 47th Super Bowl needed

Linebacker Ray Lewis gets fired up before the game, the last of his career. Lewis' seven total tackles were second on the Ravens, behind linebacker Dannell Ellerbe's nine. *Lloyd Fox | Baltimore Sun Photo*

to be, well, a little more electric. The lights went and put the old stadium in twilight for 34 minutes before all the necessary components could be reactivated.

What happened after that was just as otherworldly. Somehow, all that pent-up electrical energy seemed to flow right out of the Ravens and into the 49ers. The momentum shifted so fast that San Francisco was threatening to

tie the score before the end of the quarter. It took one more big red-zone stand in the final two minutes of the game and a strange voluntary safety with 4 seconds left before the celebration could finally begin.

The confetti was still floating over the field a half-hour later.

"We don't make it easy," Flacco said at the trophy presentation. "That's the way the city of Baltimore is. That's the way we are."

That makes two Lombardi Trophies during the Ravens era to go with two NFL championships and a Super Bowl title for the old Colts. The title puts a cherry on top of the five-year John Harbaugh era that has included a playoff run in every season, though nothing like this.

"Thank you, Baltimore fans, for sticking with us, for believing in us," Harbaugh said. "We all did it together. I'm talking about the

Tight end Dennis Pitta gathers a 1-yard touchdown pass from Joe Flacco midway through the second quarter. The reception and extra point gave the Ravens a 14-3 lead over the 49ers.   *Kenneth K. Lam | Baltimore Sun Photo*

fans, the players and the coaches and the organization, all the little kids wearing purple on Friday, all the little kids at Johns Hopkins Hospital that sent that video, thank you."

What a year it has been. The Ravens survived a string of significant injuries and a dramatic late-season coaching change to stage an inspiring surge that

started with a resounding regular-season victory over the defending Super Bowl champion New York Giants and featured that stunning divisional-round upset of the top-seeded Denver Broncos.

The Broncos probably were the best all-around team in the AFC, but Flacco's miracle throw to Jones in the final minute of regulation set up a heart-stopping

overtime victory that propelled the Ravens into an AFC title-game rematch with the New England Patriots. This time, they got it right, and all the stars seemed to be aligned for something even more special in New Orleans.

Who could possibly have doubted that after Lewis announced his retirement leading into the postseason and led all

Twelve years after his first Super Bowl championship, retiring linebacker Ray Lewis holds the Vince Lombardi Trophy in New Orleans. *Lloyd Fox | Baltimore Sun Photo*

defensive players with 44 tackles during the Ravens' first three playoff victories? Who could question the karma when all-everything offensive tackle Jonathan Ogden won election to the Pro Football Hall of Fame on Super Bowl Saturday?

Think about it. The first thing anyone can really remember about this season was the devastating Achilles tendon injury suffered by 2011 NFL Defensive Player of the Year Terrell Suggs, which should have been enough to scuttle a promising season once you considered the strength of the Ravens' 2012 schedule.

If anyone had told you they'd lose Lewis and cornerback Lardarius Webb to regular-season-ending injuries in the same game and then fire offensive coordinator Cam Cameron with four games to play, would you have been willing to bet a nickel on a winning season, must less one that ended up on the NFL's greatest stage?

What a year it has been for Baltimore sports fans of every stripe. The Orioles already had lifted our spirits with their amazing playoff run after a summer that also was highlighted by another record-setting performance by history's most decorated Olympian — Michael Phelps. It really doesn't get much better than that, but it just did.■

BALTIMORE'S NFL CHAMPIONSHIP HISTORY

BY MIKE KLINGAMAN, THE BALTIMORE SUN

1958 Season
Colts 23, New York Giants 17

NFL championship
Dec. 28, 1958
Yankee Stadium, New York

The NFL came of age in this game, a godsend for the league: two teams going toe-to-toe in sudden death for the championship in the media capital of the world. At day's end, all hailed Johnny Unitas, the Colts' steely quarterback who was two years removed from playing $8 sandlot games. Victory suited Baltimore, a blue-collar town in need of swagger. And it froze forever the bubble-gum-card countenances of Hall of Famers like Unitas, Lenny Moore, Raymond Berry, Gino Marchetti, Jim Parker and Art Donovan.■

Fullback Alan Ameche runs through a big hole to score the winning touchdown in sudden death and give the Colts their first NFL championship.
Associated Press Photo

1959 Season
Colts 31, New York Giants 16

NFL championship
Dec. 27, 1959
Memorial Stadium, Baltimore

Eclipsed by the 1958 game and forgotten by time, the Colts' second NFL title cemented their legacy and silenced skeptics who had called the first one a fluke. Baltimore's only football championship played before a home crowd, the game bore a partisan script. The Colts rallied from a 9-7 deficit to score 24 points in the final quarter. At the gun, fans streamed from the stands, hoisted players and grabbed souvenirs — everything from wooden planks off the Colts bench to the helmet right off Gino Marchetti's head.■

Hall of Fame quarterback Johnny Unitas scores on a 4-yard keeper around right end to put the Colts ahead 14-9 early in the fourth quarter.
Baltimore Sun Photo

BALTIMORE RAVENS

Super Bowl V
Jan. 17, 1971
Orange Bowl, Miami

1970 Season
Colts 16, Dallas Cowboys 13

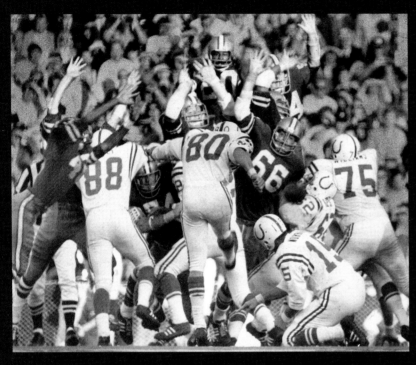

Forget the 11 turnovers, 14 penalties and slapstick surrealism that earned this Super Bowl the title of Blooper Bowl. For the Colts, victory was redemption for their upset loss to the New York Jets in Super Bowl III. With five seconds left, rookie Jim O'Brien kicked a 32-yard field goal that earned the Colts the inaugural Vince Lombardi Trophy. But their underwhelming win marked the only time in Super Bowl history that a player from the losing team (linebacker Chuck Howley) was named Most Valuable Player.■

Jim O'Brien (80) breaks a tie by kicking a 32-yard field goal with five seconds left as the Colts earn their only Super Bowl championship.
Associated Press Photo

Super Bowl XXXV
Jan. 28, 2001
Raymond James Stadium,
**   Tampa, Fla.**

2000 Season
Ravens 34, New York Giants 7

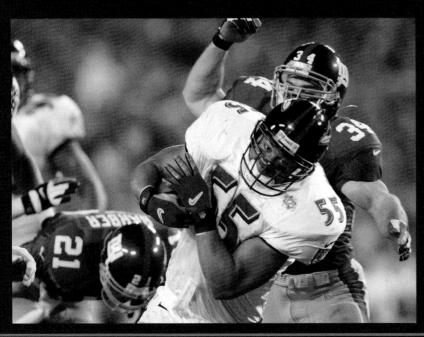

The Ravens' fifth year in the NFL and first winning season was a doozy. They won their last seven regular-season games, then ran the table in the playoffs, giving owner Art Modell the Super Bowl that had eluded him for 30 years in Cleveland. Led by a suffocating defense, the Ravens routed New York in the sixth-most one-sided Super Bowl, making converts of many die-hard Colts fans still clinging to memories of title showdowns with the Giants from a bygone era.■

Jamie Sharper runs back an interception on a ball deflected by fellow linebacker Ray Lewis in the second quarter. The Ravens picked off four passes.
Lloyd Fox | Baltimore Sun Photo

RAVENS INSIDER COVERS

SEPTEMBER 10
RAVENS 44, BENGALS 13
M&T BANK STADIUM

SEPTEMBER 16
EAGLES 24, RAVENS 23
LINCOLN FINANCIAL FIELD

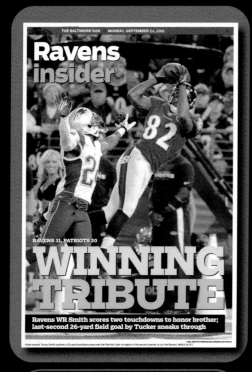

SEPTEMBER 23
RAVENS 31, PATRIOTS 30
M&T BANK STADIUM

SEPTEMBER 27
RAVENS 23, BROWNS 16
M&T BANK STADIUM

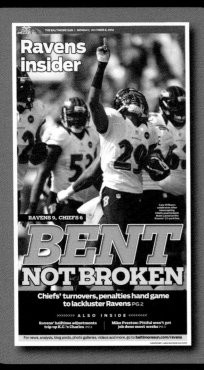

OCTOBER 7
RAVENS 9, CHIEFS 6
ARROWHEAD STADIUM

OCTOBER 14
RAVENS 31, COWBOYS 29
M&T BANK STADIUM

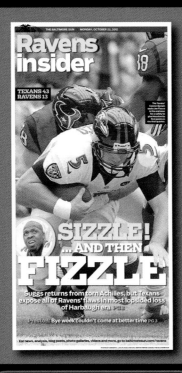

OCTOBER 21
TEXANS 43, RAVENS 13
RELIANT STADIUM

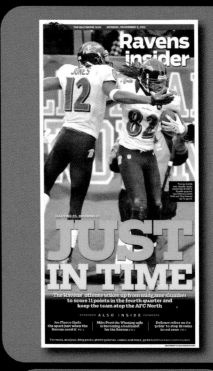

NOVEMBER 4
RAVENS 25, BROWNS 15
CLEVELAND BROWNS STADIUM

RAVENS INSIDER COVERS

NOVEMBER 11
RAVENS 55, RAIDERS 20
M&T BANK STADIUM

NOVEMBER 18
RAVENS 13, STEELERS 10
HEINZ FIELD

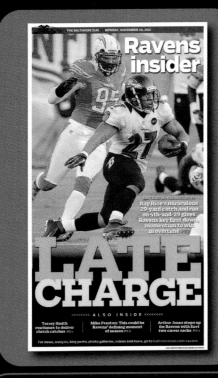

NOVEMBER 25
RAVENS 16, CHARGERS 13, OT
QUALCOMM STADIUM

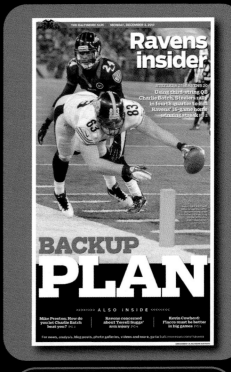

DECEMBER 2
STEELERS 23, RAVENS 20
M&T BANK STADIUM

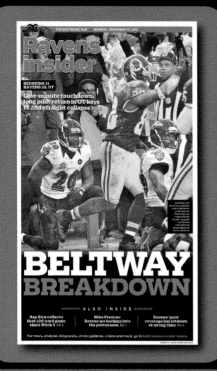

DECEMBER 9
REDSKINS 31, RAVENS 28, OT
FEDEX FIELD

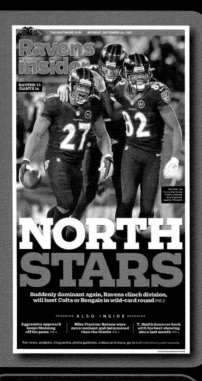

DECEMBER 16
BRONCOS 34, RAVENS 17
M&T BANK STADIUM

DECEMBER 23
RAVENS 33, GIANTS 14
M&T BANK STADIUM

DECEMBER 30
BENGALS 23, RAVENS 17
PAUL BROWN STADIUM

JANUARY 6 - AFC WILD CARD
RAVENS 24, COLTS 9
M&T BANK STADIUM

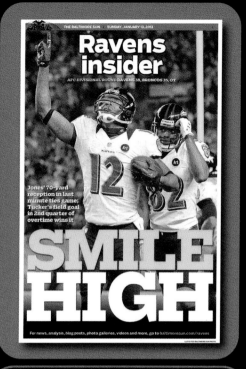

JANUARY 12 - AFC DIVISIONAL
RAVENS 38, BRONCOS 35, OT
SPORTS AUTHORITY FIELD AT MILE HIGH

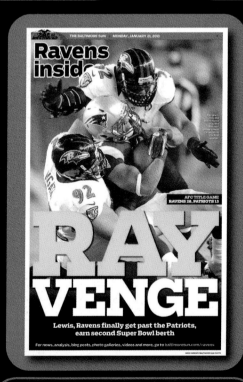

JANUARY 20 - AFC CHAMPIONSHIP
RAVENS 28, PATRIOTS 13
GILLETTE STADIUM

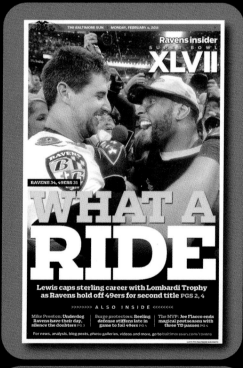

FEBRUARY 3 - SUPER BOWL
RAVENS 34, 49ERS 31
MERCEDES-BENZ SUPERDOME

baltimoresun.com   PRICE: $1.50. OUR 176TH YEAR, NO. 35

D   MONDAY, FEBRUARY 4, 2013

THE SUN

BALTIMORE
· LIGHT FOR A ·

SUPER BOWL XLVII
RAVENS 34, 49ERS 31

Champions

Ravens, up by 15 points at halftime, hold off 49ers' late-game surge to win second Super Bowl; Flacco is MVP

FULL COVERAGE
20-page Ravens insider section with analysis, statistics and more

THE CELEBRATION
Prayers and clenched fists, then cheers
NEWS PGS 6, 7

SCHMUCK
Destiny? Maybe. Undisputed champs? Definitely NEWS PG 4

GENE SWEENEY JR./BALTIMORE SUN PHOTO